Trauma *and Truce*

Personal Stories of American Veterans and Their Return to Vietnam

Colleen Woods-Esposito with Ed Woods, USMC

Foreword by Senator Thomas R. Carper, Captain, U.S. Navy (Ret.)

ISBN: 979-8-9958114-0-4

Library of Congress Control Number: 2026911068

This book includes recollections of events as they were remembered by interviewees, subjects, and participants.

In some cases, historical data, events, and other information researched by the author revealed conflicting dates, numbers, exact locations, recollections, etc. In these situations, the author has made a concerted effort to provide the most commonly held data and accounts from the most authoritative sources. The author is not a historian, and apologizes for any incorrect or disputed information or inaccuracies that have been presented.

Opinions presented by the author do not necessarily represent those of contributors, interviewees, subjects, and participants. In addition, opinions of contributors, interviewees, subjects, and participants do not necessarily represent those of the author.

Permissions pertaining to pages 230-235: PFC Edward Woods Vietnam correspondence, May 1966. Joseph Sill Clark papers (collection 1958), Historical Society of Pennsylvania.

Interior Layout and Design: Michael Ripca
Copy Editing: Karen Nolan Visconti
Cover Design: Colleen Woods-Esposito and Michael Ripca
Primary Photographers: Ed Woods and Colleen Woods-Esposito
Archival/Historical and Group Photos: Effort has been made to identify all photo sources; the publisher welcomes information to correct any omissions in future printings.

Published by Colleen-Woods Esposito
Swedesboro, New Jersey, United States of America

First Edition 2026.

This book is dedicated to all deceased Vietnam War veterans: those whose names are on the Wall in Washington D.C., and those who have died early as a result of Agent Orange exposure, war wounds, suicide, substance abuse, self-destructive behavior, and all other conditions and disorders resulting from their service. May their sacrifices never be forgotten.

You are not the darkness you endured.
You are the light that refused to
surrender.

—John Mark Green

Table of Contents

Part One: Planning and Personnel

Part Two: The Campaign

Part Three: The Debrief

Part Four: Scorched Earth

Part Five: Gathered Intelligence

Foreword

Mention the Vietnam War era to most Americans, and it brings to mind a tumultuous period of division and strife—a time whose cultural, societal, and political impact still resonates more than fifty years later.

My own connection to Vietnam began as a young Navy flight officer on the first of three deployments to Southeast Asia in 1968. Since the war, I have returned three times. The first was in 1991, when I led a bipartisan congressional delegation of veterans. Among our six members was Florida Congressman Pete Peterson, a former Air Force pilot who was shot down over North Vietnam and spent more than six years as a POW in the Hỏa Lò Prison—known to most Americans as the "Hanoi Hilton."

Our mission was twofold: to access war records on American MIAs whose bodies were never recovered, and to meet with the Prime Minister of Vietnam to explore moving toward normalized relations if the fate of the MIAs could be resolved. Those negotiations ultimately led to the recovery of hundreds of remains, and relations between our nations were fully normalized in 1995.

In 1998, as Governor of Delaware, I returned to Vietnam leading a trade delegation. In 2016, as a U.S. Senator, I visited once more—this time with President Obama—when he lifted the decades-long arms embargo, announced new economic and defense agreements, and raised important issues of human rights and protections.

Each visit was transformative, both as a veteran and as a public servant. What surprised me most were the extraordinary changes that had taken place—not least of all, the absence of hostility toward Americans. These changes have allowed our two nations to pursue shared interests and new partnerships. They also made me realize that, for some American veterans, returning to a peaceful Vietnam could provide a long-sought sense of closure and healing.

The war left an indelible mark on an entire generation of Americans. Those who fought and returned were profoundly changed, yet often lacked the support they needed to reintegrate into civilian life.

There were no homecoming parades like those given to soldiers of previous wars, and in some communities, returning veterans faced social stigma, guilt, and ostracism. Many struggled with severe psychological trauma, including undiagnosed Post-Traumatic Stress Disorder—a condition not officially recognized until 1980. Others suffered from physical wounds, Agent Orange exposure, or traumatic brain injuries, and found it difficult to access even the limited benefits available to them.

Society's failure to acknowledge veterans' experiences and sacrifices created a deep sense of betrayal among many who served. They faced unemployment, family strain, divorce, and homelessness. Their inability to readjust to life at home often led to depression, anxiety, substance abuse, and addiction. Many carried these invisible wounds for decades. Some still do.

Trauma and Truce is the chronicle of a different kind of homecoming. It tells the story of veterans returning to the country that defined their lives in ways both seen and unseen. For some, this journey was a pilgrimage toward personal peace or a confrontation with ghosts of the past. For others, it was an opportunity to experience the beauty of a land and culture they had once only seen ravaged by war. For family members accompanying them, it was a chance to better understand the experiences that shaped their loved ones. For all, it was an act of profound courage.

In addition to their return journey, this book shares wartime stories and reflections that rarely appear in history books. These first-hand accounts allow readers to better understand the extraordinary circumstances these veterans faced—and to connect with their humanity and sacrifice.

This time, they returned not to fight, but to remember, to reconcile, and to reclaim a measure of peace that had been elusive for too long. They came back to a country transformed—no longer a war zone, but a place of bustling markets, modern cities, resilient people, and stunning landscapes. Like me, I hope you'll be moved by their stories—by the moments when veterans meet former enemies who are now fellow grandfathers, and by their joy at the warm welcome extended to them and their families.

I hope this journey, so honestly and vividly told in *Trauma and Truce*, offers a sense of shared experience and healing to anyone who carries Vietnam within them—not just the veterans, but also their families and the generations who have inherited the war's legacy.

Senator Thomas R. Carper, *Captain, U.S. Navy (Ret.)*

Preface

I've always had a desire to visit Vietnam. I love the food (it's second only to my beloved Italian cuisine), and have been interested in the country's culture and history since studying the Vietnam War in high school. The enormous contrast between the hellish war experienced by a generation of young soldiers and the modern-day images of tranquil vistas and cosmopolitan cities also lured me. Time had changed this place throughout my lifetime, and something in me wanted to see the result of that transformation.

But I mostly wanted to go because my dad is a Vietnam War Marine infantry combat veteran.

Dad barely spoke about the War when I was growing up. Both his father and my mom's father were also veterans, but of that great era, World War II. The one everyone just referred to as "The War." Those guys were celebrated heroes, and could talk openly about their experiences, defeating the Nazis and the other Axis powers and saving Europe and the free world from fascism. Not that those veterans weren't affected or didn't suffer from PTSD and other psychological ailments that altered the rest of their lives. But at that time, especially during the early to mid 1970s when the Vietnam War was still raging and then still raw in the psyche of Americans, many vets chose to try and "move on" and not acknowledge the "dark demon" they rarely spoke of—a better analogy than the more common "elephant in the room."

Because for many, the Vietnam War wasn't a huge, lumbering, in-your-face animal trumpeting for recognition. It was a malevolent force that hid in the shadows and threatened to be around every corner. The dark demon was also present to veterans' families, but rarely mentioned, and only briefly in hushed tones, for fear that openly speaking of it would give it the power and force it needed to bring a person down. For me, even a person as strong as my dad.

I knew that returning to Vietnam, even decades later, would resurface some of the experiences my dad had buried. To me, being in these places and experiencing his reactions might allow me to further understand the past that helped define his character. Also, going with a small group of veterans took the visit to a higher level—one of necessity and reverence.

I've always been a writer—both as a means of self-expression and later as a means of earning a paycheck—so writing this book about our trip wasn't a far leap. My dad is a retired photographer and has also wielded the pen from time to time, so I approached him with the idea of this collaboration.

Although the process of putting together this book has sometimes been emotionally draining and overwhelming, it has been an amazingly gratifying experience that has allowed me to see a part of my dad's life that I had only previously glimpsed. It has also given me the opportunity to travel with a handful of veterans and delve into their service backgrounds, their current lives, their personal reflections about the War, and experience first-hand their return to a country that helped define them. It has allowed me to learn about the fascinating country of Vietnam and its people, the War, PTSD, and given me a deep sense of admiration and respect for the young men and women who leave the ghosts of their childhoods in the blighted landscapes of war.

While many veterans have no interest in returning to Vietnam, to those few who do, one might ask, why wait more than 50 years? There are multiple reasons, and indeed some have returned sooner.

Primarily, I believe that many Vietnam veterans are finally being properly recognized for their sacrifices. I don't mean merely a "thank you for your service" statement or a cascade of yellow ribbons–albeit those are nice gestures. Willing and able Vietnam veterans are finally receiving the full range of physiological and psychological healthcare they require to come to terms with how the War has affected their lives. The U.S. Department of Veterans Affairs (VA) has also noted that some activities that align with getting older—such as retirement, health changes, and reduction in alcohol use—can exacerbate PTSD symptoms or even trigger other war-related psychological stress.

Whether the effects of aging have led some to seek long-overdue assistance, or if such care is simply becoming more available, this trend seems to coincide with a small minority choosing to revisit

Vietnam. Some are curious. What does the country look like now? How has it changed? Some may just want to go on an exotic Asian vacation. But for all those vets who choose to go back, I believe it's also part of their journey to understanding the profound effect that the War has had on their lives and the lives of their loved ones.

Although most unfortunate are the untreated conditions of many Vietnam veterans, the reality is that it is simply too late for many to return to Vietnam, even if they ever held such a notion. Many veterans over 75 years old (some disabled) no longer have the physical ability to trek to the remote former military sites and endure the long-haul flights and other travel challenges consistent with such a visit. In addition, our 16-day tour consisted of a fast-paced and jam-packed itinerary that would have been exhausting at any age—and it needed to be, for us to complete our mission of getting a true second glance of the country. Fortunately—despite the passage of time and the physical (and sometimes psychological) challenges of the trip—all six of our veterans experienced an educational, healing, and transformative experience.

Through regular therapy and their choice to revisit Vietnam, our veteran travelers have all faced their dark demon head-on. As its features are dragged into the light and examined, the demon's power is greatly diminished. Although it will never go away completely, maybe it's not so scary any more. They can learn to live with it, and maybe even make peace with it.

Colleen Woods-Esposito
May 2026

Introduction

In almost all cases, a book can be categorized. There are fiction books such as novels or poetry, and nonfiction titles like memoirs, biographies, history, science, travel guides—the list goes on and on. But when addressing the question, what type of book are you writing, I had trouble giving a clear and concise answer.

In some ways, this book can be called a memoir, as it relays my personal story—albeit mainly as an observer and only for a short period in time. It's also an oral history of my father and the veterans I traveled with to Vietnam—but again, the time periods are limited. Although I claim to be no scholar of history or Vietnamese culture, you will also get a smidgen of those topics. Veteran-related PTSD is an overarching theme, and I have turned to the experts for medical definitions and treatments for this condition. So yes, this book covers some psychological ground, too. Vietnam is about as exotic a place as most Americans will ever read about, and this book conveys a sense of what it's like to be an American visitor. Therefore, travel is a main theme, although the purpose was unlike the leisurely holiday most plan when perusing travel guides. And while war is probably the glue that holds this book together—for without that commonality, this trip, and this book, would not have happened—it is not solely about war. Can you understand my one- or two-word categorical dilemma?

Trauma and Truce is about the life-long wounds caused by war—not only for the Marine or soldier, but for his or her family. It's about friendship and camaraderie, aging, and the search for healing and closure. It's about how the decisions of leaders and governments—often merely tactical and political to them—are intensely personal to the combat soldier. In this book, the universal search for security, freedom, and happiness is acknowledged, transcending borders to present surprising ways to define and achieve them.

Maybe it's a shortcoming that it takes multiple paragraphs to describe what this book is about. Maybe the ground I attempted to cover was too large, too daunting a task. For a long time, I was led by the nagging necessity to weave together these seemingly disjointed themes into a seamless tapestry. Eventually, I abandoned my preconceived necessity to speak in one voice. I realized that the distinct topics required different narrators: some glib and humorous, some compassionate and emotional, some swift and concise, some angry and critical, and some practical and unsentimental. My heartfelt hope is that these voices have collectively woven a meaningful and engaging narrative.

In the section "Planning and Personnel," you'll first learn how the idea for our trip to Vietnam came about and then meet our travelers by reading a bit about their backgrounds and military service. "The Campaign" chronicles our big trip, not as a strict day-by-day account of activities, but with detailed descriptions of experiences that made an impact. Our overall impressions of the trip are shared in "The Debrief." "Scorched Earth" deals with PTSD, physical wounds, and other scars of war, including contributions by a physician specialist. "Gathered Intelligence" presents our travelers' reflections on war, healing, and the human condition. This section also includes wartime testimonies from our veterans, giving you a personal account of the war experience, while hopefully illuminating the stark contrasts between the Vietnam of then and now. We conclude with a heartfelt letter to the people of Vietnam by my father, Ed Woods. Be sure to peruse our "Glossary of Terms," which includes military jargon, historical slang, and a sprinkling of Vietnamese culture, and plan to read some of the titles in the "Recommendations for Further Reading" listing.

It is my hope that, after reading this book, you come away with a deeper respect and renewed pride for war veterans, along with a lasting recognition of the profound, lifelong impact of their service. Above all, I hope you share in our group's steadfast belief in a shared humanity—regardless of the place we call home, and regardless of which government calls us to war.

Authors' Notes

What's in a Name?

The country that Americans call Vietnam is correctly spelled as two words: Việt Nam. Việt refers to the tribes or ethnic groups (Bách Việt), and Nam means South. Literally, Vietnam means Việt of the South, as in its location relative to Chinese territory. Due to its repeated use and more common spelling as one word in the United States, I will use the one-word, Westernized spelling of "Vietnam" for the purposes of this book.

In the Vietnamese language, the word "Vietnamese" changes based on whether it is used as a noun or adjective, or whether it refers to people or things. To aid my English-speaking audience, I will use the single-word form of "Vietnamese" in all these instances.

Regarding the names of cities, towns, regions, and other proper nouns, I have attempted to use the proper native spelling and diacritics (accent marks). I believe this decision will give the reader a more authentic linguistic experience, as well as respect the language.

The conflict that Americans refer to as the Vietnam War or the Vietnam Civil War, which occurred between 1955 and 1975, is referred to as the American War or the Resistance War Against America by the Vietnamese. In other parts of the world, it is often referred to as the Second Indochina War. In the interest of clarity and my largely American audience, I will be referring to the conflict as the Vietnam War.

The First Indochina War (also known as the Indochina War in France, the Anti-French Resistance War in Vietnam, and the French-Indochina War internationally) was fought in French Indochina between France and the Việt Minh Front, and its respective allies, from December 1946 until August 1954. The conflict mainly occurred in Vietnam. The Việt Minh Front was created by the Indochinese Communist Party (ICP) to achieve independence for the nation of Vietnam and later established the Democratic Republic of Vietnam (DRV), the predecessor to the modern Socialist Republic of Vietnam.

Allies and Enemies

The South Vietnamese Army, America's main ally during the War, is commonly referred to as ARVN (pronounced "arvin"), an acronym for the Army of the Republic of Vietnam. American troops used both monikers, as I do throughout this book.

Combat troops and support also came from Australia, New Zealand, and South Korea. Thailand and the Philippines provided logistical support. Throughout the book, these are included in references to "allies," "American allies," or "key allies," usually in conjunction with the South Vietnamese.

The North Vietnamese Army, one of America's enemies during the War, is usually referred to as the People's Army of Vietnam (PAVN) by historians, but was often referred to as NVA (North Vietnamese Army) by American troops. I use both throughout this book, depending on whose point of view I am reflecting.

The Việt Cong or PLAF (People's Liberation Armed Forces) was the guerrilla military force that worked in conjunction with its political arm, the National Liberation Front (NLF). Việt Cong is short for Vietnamese Communist, and this group, along with the NVA, was one of America's enemies during the War. I have primarily used the term Việt Cong, but also refer to them with the common monikers "The Cong," "Charlie," and the acronym VC.

The Draft Lottery

The veterans who were interviewed for this book—both those who traveled with us and those who did not—either volunteered or were drafted. Although the circumstances for each are described in their personal bios, I feel it necessary to explain the conditions of the draft.

During the Vietnam "Conflict," there was a legal "peacetime draft," as the U.S. Congress never formally declared war on North Vietnam.

According to the *Army University Press*, although 25 percent of the American military force in Vietnam combat zones were draftees, the lack of choices they faced after being drafted (including which military branch they would be placed in) caused many young men to volunteer.

While the National Draft *Lottery* for Vietnam began in 1969, the Selective Service relied on thousands of local autonomous draft boards to choose and notify draftees by mail from 1964-1969. That system was not random; men between the ages of 18 and a half and up to age 26 were ranked, with the oldest being chosen first to minimize disruption to education and early career development. The national lottery was introduced specifically because the previous system was considered unfair and inequitable, particularly favoring those with college deferments.

On December 1, 1969, the first draft lottery since 1942 began and was conducted by the Selective Service in Washington, D.C. The lottery was televised live, and millions of Americans watched. The lottery was a random drawing of birth dates that determined the order of military service for men born between 1944 and 1950.

Three-hundred and sixty-six blue plastic capsules containing a birth date for each day of the year were placed in a glass container. The capsules were drawn by hand and opened in order of the draw. The date on the capsule determined the lottery number for men born on that date. When men shared a birthday, the order was determined by a separate drawing of each letter of the alphabet, which were applied to the initials of their first, middle, and last names.

The first date drawn was September 14, which was assigned "001," followed by April 24, which was assigned "002," respectively. The process continued until each day of the year was assigned a number.

Draft lotteries were conducted again in 1970, 1971, and 1972, with the last group drafted on December 7, 1972.

The United States military drafted approximately 2.2 million American men into their ranks between 1964 and 1973, out of an eligible pool of 27 million. Of the 27 million eligible, 8.7 million volunteered for service.

About 17,671 draftees died in the Vietnam War, which was about 30% of the total 58,220 U.S. military members who died in the conflict.

Millions of young men tried to evade the draft. Various exemptions included college deferments and being declared physically or mentally unfit. Some fled to Canada and some used family connections to secure safe positions in the National Guard. This allowed for those of higher socio-economic status and better connections to evade the draft more easily than working class or minority men. Most sources estimate that about 80% of U.S. troops in the War came from working-class and lower-income families.

A Note on the Draft by Ed Woods

The military draft brought the War to the American home front. At the height of the War in 1968, the Marine Corps was included in the draft system. But during my time in Vietnam between 1965-66, no Marines were drafted.

The draft was a necessary evil. We were at war, with mounting losses of troops to serious injury and death. As Marines, we all wanted to be there. The thought of serving with conscripts was not appealing to us at all. At the base in Đà Nẵng, we would interact with Army personnel during downtime. I was never involved in any discussion of the draft with anyone. However, the Army guys seemed to complain more.

Of greater interest was the difference in our rifles. We had the heavier M14, while the Army soldiers carried the lighter, newer M16. The M14, firing a heavier 7.62mm NATO round, was known for its accuracy and stopping power, whereas the M16, using a smaller 5.56mm round, offered greater mobility and allowed for carrying more ammunition. Although we were envious of the extra ammo they could carry, "stopping power" was the magic phrase for me.

Weapons varied, and the advantages and disadvantages can be debated. But we Marines, at least during my time, wanted to be there. The Army draftees didn't. That was the big difference.

Part One

Planning and Personnel

Our group enters the Imperial City of Huế.

Now, every time I witness a strong person, I want to know: What darkness did you conquer in your story? Mountains don't rise without earthquakes.

—Katherine MacKenett

An About Face

It began a few years ago, before the pandemic. I told my Dad about an article I had read concerning a group of veterans going back to tour Vietnam and how that might be something good for him. I also knew he liked to travel, and had organized both civilian and veteran tours of European destinations.

His response was quick: I'd rather stick a knife in my eye.

When my Dad says something definitive like that, in that tone, I know not to push it. So that was the end of the discussion.

I was pretty surprised a few months later when my Dad mentioned that he was thinking about taking a group of war veterans to Vietnam.

Apparently, the idea stuck with him and needed time to marinate a bit, because he mentioned it to his veteran PTSD group therapist, who told him that it could be part of a healing process to return to a place of trauma under new circumstances, or something to that effect. Turns out that same therapist even came on our trip. But I'll get to that.

During January and February of 2020, Dad was planning his solo "recon" trip, a process where he goes to a destination first to check out the area, hotels, and so forth before taking a group. He found a Vietnamese travel professional to help him develop an itinerary and provide guides. He bought his plane tickets.

A month later, the pandemic hit.

The long and uncertain time of Covid-19 enveloped us, and the trip was all but forgotten. We buckled down and did our best to stay healthy. After the first Coronavirus lull, the variant resurgence, reopened borders, closed entries, booster shots, and anti-vaxxers, the virus was finally no longer the focus of everyone's life. Good riddance.

Then I asked my dad in mid 2022, are you still planning that trip to Vietnam? Hell yeah, he was.

My dad originally planned his recon trip back alone. Since the rest of the family was a bit nervous about a solo jaunt, and my mom was planning on going on the group trip, my brother decided to accompany Dad on the recon.

So, in October of 2022, my dad and brother took off for Vietnam.

Reconnaissance

My dad and brother did not visit the areas where Dad fought and was stationed during the War—around Đà Nẵng in the central part of the country. Dad did not want to travel to those sites twice; he wanted to revisit them for the first time with the other veterans. Understandable. This first trip would cover the north around Hà Nội and into the mountains, as well as the south into Sài Gòn and the Mekong Delta.

Even so, I thought my dad would be nervous about his first trip back to a country that defined his transformation from a naïve teenager into a seasoned fighter, a place where he experienced trauma and his childhood truly ended. But when I asked him about it, he told me that he was not apprehensive because he had a mission: to set up the trip for the veterans. That is where his military mind took over, more than 50 years later.

Dad's mission helped him focus on what he needed to do and kept his mind off negative thoughts. Oh, the irony of this. I was beginning to fully understand how the military worked—how it encompassed the entire soldier, the entire human being—past, present, and future. My dad is a Marine. I say *is* a Marine, not *was* a Marine, because, "Once a Marine, always a Marine." On the surface, that quote may seem merely a branch euphemism (along with "Semper Fi" which means *always faithful*, the Marine Corps loyalty motto). But that's not all it is. The completion and success of each mission, the following of orders without debate, the consciousness of always being on guard, or "watching your six"—they never go away. The training and wartime experiences of a combat veteran

Ed and his son, Eddie, are shown here at the Stone Gate of Vietnam's ancient capital, Hoa Lư, in Ninh Bình Province.

take root so deep in the psyche that they never cease to be part of their identity.

I asked if being back among Vietnamese people made him feel threatened. He said his guard is up at all times at home, so it wasn't any more than usual. So, although my dad's first return visit was mainly a positive planning-based recon visit, it was a vacation, too.

Dad did share one experience that brought back a vivid and traumatic war memory. Vietnam in general—and especially Hà Nội—is a place populated by young people in their late teens and early twenties, the same age as many of the enemies American troops fought during the War. Young Vietnamese males not in uniform often wore white, short-sleeved, button-down shirts at that time. When Dad arrived in Hà Nội on this return trip, he was surrounded by young people, and soon saw a young man in a white button-down shirt. He told me he felt a deep sense of uneasiness regarding those white shirts.

Dad proceeded to tell me a story that he's decided not to share in this book. Some things need to remain private, or shared with only a trusted few.

He's only ever told me a handful of profound stories. Sometimes they come out of nowhere, when the War or being a Marine is never even a point of discussion. And even though we were discussing the War this time, these experiences are so contradictory to the teenage reality that I experienced, that they never cease to shock me.

I wonder what it would be like to have had the traumatic experiences that he's had. The reliving of those moments in my mind, year after year, decade after decade. How would I have coped?

I am in awe of my dad and the strength he has. He's a rough and tough old Marine, and I don't just mean physically. The stuff he's experienced would send lesser minds into a straitjacket. I know it hasn't been easy for him: he has extreme hypervigilance due to PTSD, which he's only had diagnosed over the past decade. He went through years of anger issues, self-medicating, and everything else that goes along with the diagnosis. And that's just the mental part.

I think about the 18-year-olds I know and I can't imagine them ever emerging from such life-altering trauma. Don't get me

The Presidential Palace in Hà Nội was designed and built by French colonists in the early 1900s. Hồ Chí Minh refused to live in this lavish palace, using it only for official business.

wrong, Dad did not emerge unscathed. But not long after the War, he became a loving husband and father and worked a steady job. I suppose he learned to compartmentalize, as they say. Sometimes things were tough, but he kept trucking along. As much as I admire today's youth—their sense of community, acceptance, and passion for positive change—it took a grittier generation with unwavering resilience to come out the other end of what my dad went through. Or perhaps all generations have the ability to rise to the level of their distinctive challenges.

Upon landing in Vietnam after a 14-hour flight, with his spinal column stiff and aching, my brother considered our dad's thoughts during this long flight in 1964. He was headed to the other side of the world, to a place where the people looked different, spoke differently, and were unsure why the Americans were there. Also, the prospect of not coming home was real and frightening.

My brother said that the people of Vietnam made the trip special.

He knew that our dad wanted to come back to see them in a different light, and he did. As visitors, they were always treated with respect and, in some cases, reverence. At a remote floating village, the young women wanted their pictures taken with the light-

Ed and his son Eddie enjoy "fresh beer" (draught) on Beer Street in Hà Nội.

skinned, freckled Americans. My brother laughed and said that they are probably featured on a few Vietnamese teenagers' Instagram accounts.

My father and brother learned how a society can live on very little, yet still be very happy. In contrast, we Americans often believe that having more will make us happier. My brother also realized that the Vietnamese people saw Westerners as generous and accepting of other cultures.

Upon returning from his recon trip, my dad created a beautiful, comprehensive slideshow and told stories about the villages, cities, traffic, food, and friendly locals. He shared it with the other vets in his therapy groups, piquing their interest even further. A group of travelers began to form, and the veterans' return trip soon became a reality.

Our dad seemed to make peace with the past, even on this reconnaissance trip. There was no war, there was no death. There were no enemies, only new friends. It began a period of catharsis and healing that we hoped would be reaffirmed on his second visit with other veterans.

Meet the Troops

Lou Garrison

Louis Harry Garrison was born in 1945 and grew up in Pennsylvania and New Jersey. His dad was a World War II veteran who later built his career contracting farmers to supply produce for Campbell's Soup. His mom took care of the three kids and the home, and also worked part-time as a cashier at Lou's high school cafeteria in Glassboro, New Jersey.

Lou never liked school, had lousy grades, and seemed to maybe have a problem with authority. As a result, he was shipped down to Florida Military School in DeLand, Florida. Not surprisingly, he didn't like it. But, also not surprisingly, he got used to it and then liked it—enough to graduate then enter the college branch of the school until it closed in 1966.

Lou transferred to Delaware Valley College in Doylestown, Pennsylvania to finish his degree. He continued to be a poor student grade-wise, and his father told him to stick it out as long as he could, or at least until he got kicked out. After all, boys his age were getting drafted and shipped off to Vietnam. He chose to stick it out and graduated in 1969 with a degree in horticulture.

Lou was working at a nearby farm when his draft lottery number came up later that year. He reported to the recruitment station in Woodbury, New Jersey, where the recruiters lined everyone up. Every fourth guy was sent to the Marine Corps, the rest to the Army. Lou went to the Army, where he was offered advanced training due to his college degree. But because that training required a longer commitment, Lou took the regular grunt path.

Lou couldn't escape the draft. He was going to 'Nam.

After basic training at Fort Dix, New Jersey, and advanced infantry training at Fort McClellan, Alabama, Lou was able to go home for about a week to celebrate Christmas with his family. Would it be his last? He flew to an oversees replacement station in California, and three days later was shipped directly to Vietnam on a civilian jet. It was January of 1970.

It's been over 50 years since Lou fought in the War, and he's suffered from strokes. He emphasized that he may have forgotten some things, especially some details. But the big things stay with him.

Lou flew into the Long Bình "Redcatchers" Army Combat Training Center, where he stayed for a couple days, then moved on to Fire Support Base (FSB) Nancy where he was stationed as part of the U.S. Army's 199th Light Infantry Brigade. As a firebase, Nancy was used to provide support (usually artillery) to infantry operating beyond the normal range of their base camps. Along with U.S. Army brigades, Nancy (later known as Mỹ Chánh) also supported Republic of Vietnam (ARVN) troops. The base was located 9 kilometers (14 miles) southeast of the village of Quảng Trị and northwest of Huế in central Vietnam. Today, the area is farmland.

When Lou was stationed at Nancy, he would not have been able to tell you the location. He wasn't sure where he was, and as private, he did not need to know. He just needed to follow his orders. Such was the life of an infantry solider.

As part of the 199th Light Infantry Brigade, Lou often traveled by foot through the jungle, usually with his company. Companies operated under battalions within the brigade, subdivided into platoons and then squads, which typically included seven to 10 soldiers. Sometimes Lou went out with smaller squads in trucks or helicopters. As the groups moved along, they usually camped overnight, as missions lasted 10 days to two weeks. At the end of a mission, they'd return to base, get showers, eat decent meals, and two to three days later would be back out again. While at FSB Nancy between missions, troops provided security for the base.

Missions usually began with the company being dropped at point A and proceeding to point B to see what they could find. Lou said that they were looking to make contact, kind of like looking for trouble. Sometimes they found it, and engaged the enemy, who was typically the Việt Cộng. Fortunately for Lou, his company commander had previously served as a medic and refused to let the troops walk on established trails, as that was where they found *too much* trouble. Instead, Lou spent a lot of time cutting through thorny jungle to avoid ambushes. He wasn't even issued a machete, but relied entirely on a bowie knife sent by his father.

One day in June or July of 1970, Lou was ordered to set an ambush using Claymore mines. These mines are command-detonated (fired by remote control) or activated by a booby-trap trip wire. Being highly directional, they shoot a wide pattern of steel balls into a designated kill zone when fired.

On this day, Lou had done most of the work setting the mines, which resulted in injuring or killing some enemies. But some were still alive, and a firefight ensued, where Lou's squad killed the rest. Because they had made so much noise, Lou's squad moved a mile away, where he was ordered to set more mines. While setting a mine, a blasting cap detonated, blowing off the fingers of Lou's left hand. Fortunately, the cap was not yet placed in the mine, so Lou only received damage from the cap, not the entire explosive. He would not be alive to tell this story if the mine had been fully set.

A medic wrapped Lou's hand, but knowing it would get infected easily, his company commander called for a medevac. A helicopter arrived and lowered a seat for him so he could be hoisted into the chopper. Lou ended up at a medical camp that he said reminded him of M*A*S*H. The staff treated his hand as best they could, but he was eventually transferred via a C-130 turbo and then another helicopter to Camp Zama Army hospital in Japan.

There, x-rays revealed that only tendon was still attached, rendering his hand largely unusable. Lou is forever grateful for Major Gross (his surgeon), who gave him the choice to either reconstruct his hand (to make it look normal) or have it amputated. Lou chose to undergo several operations to save it. To this day, Lou's hand looks normal unless examined up close. He has no use of his pinky and very minimal use of his other fingers. Later, as a civilian, Lou mostly had trouble throwing change into the toll gate bucket when commuting to his job. It's a shame E-ZPass wasn't around for most of his career.

After his hand operations, Lou flew on a C-141 Starlifter from Japan to Alaska, then to McGuire Air Force Base in New Jersey where he spent at least three months at Walson Army Hospital in Fort Dix. Lou also had some cap fragments in his chest, but they worked their way out on their own.

Even if you get injured in the line of duty, you still have to fulfill your time commitment. Lou finished his duty at the Fort Dix finance department. He reported to officers and MPs who handled base payroll. It was light duty, and Lou had a car.

Lou was discharged on August 6, 1971, a month early, as he was asked to help his former employer, Petane Brothers Farms, with the harvest. Lou received a "regular" discharge, DD-214. His rank began as an E-2 (Private), and he finished as an E-4 (Specialist).

Lou's stint in Vietnam was over, and he resumed his life as a civilian.

Putting his college degree to use, Lou got a job with the U.S. Department of Agriculture. He inspected produce—cherries, corn, and tomatoes.

In July 1974, Lou married Karen Kruse, a second-grade teacher who later received her doctorate in education. When they met, she was dating his best friend, Mike. Everyone remained friends, and Mike was even the best man at Lou and Karen's wedding.

Lou and Karen have two children: Sean, born in 1980, and Siobhan, born in 1983.

Lou remained in the agricultural realm, later taking a job as manager at the New Jersey Apple Industry Council, and retired in 2008 from banana importers M. Levin & Company, Inc. Karen retired in 2010. The two retirees enjoy their beautiful property in Washington Township, New Jersey, and travel as much as they can.

Lou chuckled and said he goes to therapy because his wife told him to. However, having been fired from so many jobs over the years, he also suspected something else was going on.

At his discharge in 1971, Lou was rated as a 10% disabled veteran, but he is now at 100%. He started going to the VA after 40 years when he learned he had a purple heart claim to process, so he went in and filled out the paperwork.

As Vietnam is a big part of his past, Lou wanted his wife Karen to see it, and they both joined us on the trip. Lou was also curious what it looks like without the helicopters, artillery, and mortar fire. And he wanted to know what it smells like now.

Lou was considering going to Vietnam on his own, just him and Karen, but found out from his therapist about our group trip. He did not know my dad beforehand. The couple's prior international travels have included a visit to Israel and a cruise around Cuba.

Lou said he was not nervous about returning to Vietnam, citing one distinct advantage: having had three mini-strokes, he remembers little about his time there. Yet, like many of the vets I've interviewed, the more we spoke, the more the memories resurfaced.

Raymond Kennedy

Born in 1950, Ray grew up in Bellmawr, New Jersey, one of four siblings and the only one to have served in the military. Ray's family was very poor and lived on a houseboat that was pulled onto dry land until 1956, when his father built a house next to the boat. Neither structure had running water until 1963, when Ray was 13.

After graduating from Triton High School in 1968, Ray began working for South Jersey Paving in Chews Landing, New Jersey. He drove rock trucks and other heavy equipment, transporting gravel to the sand plant. About a year later, he began driving earth movers at Buzby Brothers Materials Pit in Gibbsboro, New Jersey.

Ray knew the draft was coming for him, not only because the War was escalating but also because he had a low number in the draft lottery, making him likely to get shipped out sooner than most. In June of 1971, Ray received his draft notice. He was 20 years old.

Ray says he wasn't scared when he was drafted, realizing he had no choice and just needed to take one day at a time. While this may sound like a case of false bravado, if you knew Ray, you'd believe him. His easy, calm demeanor is one of the strongest facets of his personality. Even in the throes of youth, I believe Ray was a chill dude.

During basic training at Fort Dix, New Jersey, Ray's top testing scores and high IQ earned him a spot in warrant officer flight school, which would have qualified him to fly light aircraft and helicopters. However, after discovering it required an additional two-year time commitment, he declined. Like many draftees, Ray wasn't one of those gung-ho guys itching to fight.

For the first six months in-country, Ray was stationed with the 554th Engineers in Bảo Lộc, a mountaintop basecamp in the central highlands of Lâm Đồng Province, about 182 kilometers (113 miles) northeast of Sài Gòn.

Although Ray left for Vietnam with an MOS of 62-E20—a bulldozer operator—he never ran a dozer the entire time he was in 'Nam. In Bảo Lộc, he was given an S-2 security and intelligence assignment. Most days consisted of Ray and his sergeant driving around the base perimeter to make sure no enemies had cut the wire and snuck into the base. They would also go to "ARVN"—the South Vietnamese Army Headquarters—to obtain intelligence reports on enemy troop strength and movements, particularly the VC. Such is the changing nature of wartime—you go where you are needed and do what you are told.

When the engineers in Ray's company finished the transport highway they were building, they returned to the States. Since Ray's in-country time commitment was shy by four months, he was reassigned to the 1st Air Cavalry Division at Long Bình Post, a large combined Army and Air Force base about 20 kilometers (12 miles) northeast of Sài Gòn. The post was also home to the notorious Long Bình Stockade military prison, where a 1968 race-related riot occurred.

Although his job remained S-2 security and intelligence, Ray was often sent on five- to seven-day recon missions with four others, including an ARVN scout. He also periodically retrieved supplies in Sài Gòn for the officers' clubs on the base.

Ray's recon missions sometimes sent him into Cambodia. On one of those occasions, he was hit with shrapnel under the chin. Even though he was injured, Ray could not receive a purple heart or recognition because all missions to Cambodia were classified.

In April 1972, Ray received his discharge orders. He left Vietnam and the Army. There was no welcoming committee for Ray, but there was his family.

After returning home, Ray filed a UCX claim and received unemployment benefits for a short time. He then worked various jobs, including general construction and contracting, driving trucks for asphalt and septic companies, and working on storm drains, water mains, and water towers. Ray said that despite working all these jobs, he struggled to cope with people.

Finally, Ray found his place in the West Deptford Art Guild as a union carpenter and stayed for the remainder of his career. During his time at the Guild, Ray helped build the Des Moines children's museum and the NBC studio for the 2004 Olympics in Athens, Greece. He retired in 2012.

Ray has two children and two grandchildren, all of whom live nearby. In July 2016, his wife of 23 years, Katarina, a German national, passed away from congestive heart failure. She was 66.

In retirement, Ray enjoys spending time with the grandkids and making and repairing custom fishing rods and reels.

After retiring, Ray lost his health insurance. Realizing his time in Vietnam had taken a toll on his health, he now receives health care and a disability check each month from the VA. Ray thanks God for the VA.

The VA has rated Ray as a 100% disabled veteran, with diagnoses of PTSD, diabetes, hearing loss, and—most recently recognized as service-related—bladder cancer. Ray also suffers from tremors which are currently being monitored by his VA doctors, but are not classified as service-related at the time of this writing.

Although diagnosed with PTSD due to the trauma he experienced in Vietnam, Ray prefers to keep those experiences private.

He was not nervous about returning to Vietnam, and his family reacted positively to the idea, so he decided to join our trip.

Kevin Laughlin

Kevin was born in 1948 in Kenmore, New York, a suburb of Buffalo. He experienced early trauma caused by his alcoholic father,

whose car accident killed Kevin's seven-year-old sister. Within a year, his parents divorced. Because Kevin's mother held a college degree, she secured a job teaching high school English and Latin.

Supporting nine children on her own, Kevin's mother decided she could not immediately care for the youngest, so five-year-old Kevin and his younger brother, Michael, were sent to an orphanage without explanation. They remained there for a year before their uncle took them in as foster children.

Unfortunately, conditions weren't much better there. Kevin and his brother Michael were bullied by their older cousins and attended a rough inner-city parochial school. After three years with their uncle, Kevin and Michael moved back home with their mother, who was by then settled into her job. They kept busy with household chores and, for a time, worked in the basement when not at school to support the family's egg-candling business (the process of placing a candle behind an egg to observe embryo development, now done with modern lighting equipment).

After finishing eighth grade, Kevin enrolled in the Diocesan Preparatory Seminary, where he finished high school and attended two years of their college program. However, working as a bartender, drinking, partying, and dating made Kevin realize the priesthood was not for him, so he transferred to Canisius University, a Jesuit college in downtown Buffalo.

By then, the Vietnam War was in full swing, and Kevin's brother Michael was drafted and accepted into officer candidate school. In 1969, while Michael was in Vietnam, Kevin joined a Buffalo, New York protest against the illegal bombing of Cambodia.

In 1970, Kevin graduated with a bachelor's degree in English. He knew he'd be drafted since his birthdate was pulled as number six in the live TV lottery. The dates were printed on balls, which is where the use of ping-pongs balls for the lottery originated. Kevin jokingly noted that it was the only lottery he ever won. It was later discovered that they did not mix the balls well, and the first four months of the year were getting pulled more often. Kevin was born in April.

Knowing his draft was looming, Kevin visited a recruiter to delay entry so he could spend the summer with his brother, Michael, who was returning home from combat duty. Kevin was offered a three-year Army optical laboratory specialist role (in essence, an eyeglass maker). The two brothers went on a fishing vacation in Canada, where Michael tried to convince Kevin to stay, but Kevin wanted to fulfill his duty. Besides, the recruiter told Kevin that his chances of going to Vietnam were slim to none with his eyeglass-making assignment. (Oh, those recruiters and their fibs.)

After six months of training in Colorado, Kevin was stationed at the Tracy Supply Depot in California, where he had his first of many run-ins with his superiors. When their captain berated Kevin for being covered in eyeglass polishing material and another soldier for being overweight, the pair stopped work in protest, not something the Army takes kindly to.

Kevin's problem with authority continued when he reached Vietnam in mid-1971 and was told his job classification wasn't needed. Kevin responded by calling his Lieutenant Colonel a "dumb son-of-a-bitch," and paid for that insubordination by completing a full year in Vietnam. He was assigned to the 95th Evacuation Hospital in Đà Nẵng, and was finally able to make some eyeglasses. Along with those duties, he operated the x-ray machine, provided security, and transported burn patients as a medevac driver. Kevin remained in the area for his full year, including an assignment at the Đà Nẵng airbase when his hospital closed.

Upon returning to the U.S., Kevin spent eight months at Fort Dix to finish his service, where he continued making eyeglasses. There, he met Dr. Mary Zelanis, who later became his wife. Even at

Fort Dix, Kevin could not escape trouble. He was reprimanded for taking unauthorized leave and was pulled from his lab to perform eye exams for trainees. Kevin's struggle with authority continued when he defied a drill sergeant who refused to allow trainees waiting for screenings to get a drink of water in 95-degree heat.

Kevin was nervous, jumpy, and reactive to noise after being in Vietnam. His alcohol problem grew.

Kevin and Mary were married in 1974 and settled in Vineland, New Jersey, and Mary became a stabilizing influence. Kevin obtained his master's degree in literature and linguistics at the University of Delaware and worked as a tutor and ESL (English as a Second Language) instructor before becoming a seventh-grade English teacher in Vineland for 13 years.

In 1984, Kevin began suffering from bad headaches, and was often unable to move without being in complete agony. Local doctors told him it was "all in his head," and would not give him a prescription for the pain. Kevin ended up spending a year moving back and forth between the Philadelphia and Wilmington VA hospitals, with Washington, D.C. specialists brought in to aid in a diagnosis.

After several tests, including an x-ray of his back that revealed a shadow, it was finally discovered that Kevin had a bone infection, and his bones were being eaten away by bacteria. While stationed in Đà Nẵng, the area around Kevin's hospital and the heliport was defoliated with Agent Orange, and the infection was attributed to this exposure. To eradicate the infection and stop the bone loss, Kevin was treated with large doses of intravenous antibiotics. During this ordeal, Kevin lost 50 pounds and two inches of height from bone compression, resulting in severe nerve pain.

Unable to have biological children, Kevin and Mary adopted 12 children over the years, from local areas and as far away as Columbia and then Russia, where Kevin was involved in a teacher exchange program.

At age 42, Kevin finally entered AA, which helped him kick the habit. He has been sober ever since.

Once sober, Kevin's ambitious nature returned, and he continued his education by earning another master's degree, this time in educational principalship from Rowan University in Glassboro, New Jersey, which helped him land a principal's position at Christiana High School in Newark, Delaware. While there, Kevin earned a Doctor of Education (EdD) from the University of Delaware. He returned to teaching for three years in Moorestown, New Jersey, as a seventh-grade English teacher before retiring in 2012.

Not one to stop the process of lifelong learning because of a small thing like retirement, Kevin then joined a six-year formation program to become a Roman Catholic deacon. During that time, he earned yet another degree—this one in spiritual counseling from Neumann University in Aston, Pennsylvania. What made this choice different from the rest was that it was inspired by his own condition.

Since his time in Vietnam, the banging of screen doors has always bothered Kevin, and the firing of guns and other loud noises during his son's U.S. Marine graduation at Parris Island was very difficult. His war nightmares returned.

In 2006, Kevin was diagnosed with PTSD at the Department of Veterans Affairs in Wilmington, Delaware, where he began receiving both group and individual therapy. Wanting to help others, Kevin put his new degree to work beginning in 2011, eventually evaluating over 300 veterans while working for Family and Psychological Services Inc., which held a grant through the state of New Jersey. However, the process of treating veterans was adversely affecting his own PTSD recovery. Consequently, Kevin began working as a volunteer in 2018, counseling mostly non-veteran patients, although he still holds one group therapy session for veterans.

Kevin is classified as a 100% disabled veteran by the VA, and joined our trip as both a traveling vet and group therapist. From a personal perspective, he was curious to see how the country of Vietnam is faring and wanted to find out firsthand what impact the War had on the country. He was not nervous about returning to Vietnam itself, but was concerned about the length of the long-haul flights.

As a current therapist to some of our vets, Kevin also wanted to support their visit by coming along. During the trip, he met regularly with all the veterans to monitor their reactions and mental states, addressing the questions and concerns of everyone in our group.

We travelers are eternally grateful for Kevin's expertise and compassion before, during, and after our travels.

Charles Walter

Born October 16, 1942, Charles Walter grew up as the only child of a general contractor father and a mother who worked as a cashier at a Philadelphia Sheraton hotel. The family resided in Camden, New Jersey, where Charles graduated from Woodrow Wilson High School in 1961.

After receiving a certificate in electrical technology from Temple University in 1965, Charles worked at the Camden shipyard before enlisting in the Army in 1966. Like many young men of that era, he knew enlisting offered advantages over being drafted, such as the ability to choose his military branch and, most likely, his specific assignment.

Charles attended basic training at Fort Dix before being shipped to the now-defunct Fort Monmouth in New Jersey to study air defense radar for 34 weeks. Following a two-month stint at the Michigan Arsenal Base in Detroit, he was sent to Fort Bliss, Texas, to study the IFF (Identification Friend or Foe) radar reading system. Charles still recalls the white sands of Texas, where the Army tested short-range missiles equipped with warheads.

He was hoping that the War would end during his training, but it kept raging.

Although Charles had bad allergies, he could not get a medical deferment; instead he was sent to Valley Forge Hospital to get desensitizing shots for ragweed, grasses, trees, cats, and dogs. The Army also supplied him with vials of weekly shots in dry ice to take to Vietnam, which Charles says helped quite a bit.

After his training in Texas, Charles returned to Detroit and got his orders for Vietnam. He was not happy to be going, and his parents were upset. He was sent to Fort Benning in Georgia to ship out. Charles remembers seeing the movie *The Green Berets* being filmed there, starring John Wayne. The movie was filmed as a military

propaganda tool during a time when the War was becoming increasingly unpopular.

The Army decided that Charles should also be trained in ground support radar repair (similar to the type used in airports), so his Vietnam ship-out date was delayed for five more weeks as he returned to Fort Monmouth for additional training.

Finally, in August of 1968 Charles arrived at Dầu Tiếng Base Camp, situated between the Michelin Rubber Plantation and the Sài Gòn River in Bình Dương Province. The base commanded a strategic position at the southern end of the Hồ Chí Minh Trail near the Cambodian border and enabled monitoring of the "Iron Triangle," a 193-kilometer (120-mile) enemy stronghold which included the massive Củ Chi tunnel complex. The base was also situated close to Black Virgin Mountain (Núi Bà Đen). U.S. Army Special Forces held the top of the mountain, the Việt Cộng held the middle, and the South Vietnamese Army held the base. Charles said that every once in a while, the Việt Cộng would come up and fight with the Special Forces. While protecting Sài Gòn from enemy infiltration, Dầu Tiếng's position, supply depots, and airstrip also enabled the U.S. and its allies to rush reinforcements to nearby fire-bases and active operations.

Dầu Tiếng Base was regularly referred to as Camp Rainier by American soldiers, including Charles. The moniker derived from the first U.S. Army unit that arrived from Fort Lewis, Washington, which offered views of Mt. Rainier. But this was no peaceful mountainscape in the Pacific Northwest.

Charles says he will always remember the horrible smells of death as soon as he landed.

Because he was trained for it, Charles logically thought his job would be support radar, but there were no positions available. Instead, he was assigned to work for a major and first sergeant as a company clerk for about a month, while also observing planes coming in and reporting any problems. And as per usual, with other duties as assigned.

When Charles first arrived at Camp Rainier, he was housed in the barracks. The camp was a hotbed of activity due to its position, and Charles experienced multiple rocket attacks and attempted sabotage during his time there. When a large number of grunts arrived, he was moved into one of several large houses that were part of the rubber plantation. As one might imagine, being housed in a white French Colonial mansion with plaster walls and a terra cotta roof in the middle of an active war zone was a surreal experience.

When he was finally reassigned, Charles could not leave via convoy because the base was under siege, so he was moved to the nearby Biên Hòa Airbase, roughly 25 kilometers (16 miles) from Sài Gòn. He started as a SPC4 and later was promoted to a SPC5. This means he was in charge of equipment rather than people. Army radar headquarters was located here, and after a five-week refresher course, he was finally able to perform his original assignment, a job similar to a civilian air traffic controller.

Charles moved around a bit more, first to the base above the famed Củ Chi Tunnels, which were inhabited by the Việt Cộng. There, tunnel entrances were searched out and destroyed, with brave "tunnel rat" soldiers sent on extremely harrowing and dangerous missions inside the tunnels.

Charles's final assignment was at the Ocean Base R&R Center in Sài Gòn. Along with air traffic control at these locations, he was often sent to retrieve and deliver parts for his radar.

No matter where Charles was assigned during his time in Vietnam, he never felt safe. The enemy was all around, and could be working on the base. Like most soldiers, he went to bed with a loaded firearm. Ground attacks from rockets occurred every night. Charles said many people were killed from these attacks, and some came really close to him.

There was no escape from the War, even at the R&R center, where soldiers were supposed to be able to catch a short break. While he was stationed there, the enemy placed a bomb in one of the metal mess kit containers in the chow hall, which blew up the mess area. Luckily, Charles was not there at the time. Our B-52 planes also dropped bombs at night where they thought the enemy was hiding in Sài Gòn. He recalls being at a hotel and hearing those shockwaves from a mile away.

Charles served in Vietnam for about a year total. After returning home, he worked for Diebold, Inc., starting in 1970, and decided to get another degree while working (funded by the GI Bill and his employer).

Charles and Agnes Sheraton were married in 1974. The couple has three adult children and eight grandchildren. They have lived in New Jersey since 1981.

In 1985, Charles graduated with a B.S. in engineering from Widener University in Pennsylvania. He held different positions for a total of 35 years, installing ATM machines, vaults, safes, safety deposit boxes, under-counter money equipment for banks, alarms, and security cameras. He is a proud member of IEEE (Institute of Electrical and Electronic Engineers), and retired in 2005.

Charles has been rated as a highly disabled veteran by the VA. Like all of the vets who traveled with us, Charles has PTSD. He also suffers multiple effects from Agent Orange exposure, including a diabetic thyroid condition, prostate cancer (he's in remission now but still has side effects), neuropathy (nerve damage in his hands and feet), skin cancer, hearing loss, and central sleep apnea (which differs from obstructive sleep apnea because the brain does not send proper signals to the muscles that control breathing). Charles mentioned that he received specialized care from the Philadelphia VA, which was a pioneer in sleep apnea studies.

Charles decided to join our trip to Vietnam mainly because he wanted to see how the country has changed and because he likes to travel. At the time of his interview, he had been to 21 countries, all 50 states, and most Canadian provinces.

When asked if he was nervous or anxious about returning, Charles said he had never been to the northern part of the country where some of our visits were planned. However, he'd have to wait and see what would happen when we got to Sài Gòn, where he experienced frequent bombing, and the Củ Chi tunnels, which were constantly being blown up to root out the enemy.

Charles' wife Agnes, a retired insurance clerk, also joined us on the trip.

Ed Woods

Ed was born September 1, 1946. His father was a WWII Army veteran who enlisted and was stationed as a mechanic in Guadalcanal, Solomon Islands, in the South Pacific. After the war, his dad continued as a diesel mechanic, eventually retiring from the Philadelphia Navy Yard. His mother was a homemaker and part-time salesperson, and she eventually retired as a full-time employee from the subscription department at *TV Guide*.

Ed was raised in Upper Darby, Pennsylvania, and attended Monsignor Bonner High School. He is the eldest of five children and the only son. After graduating from high school in 1964, he worked as a baker, making pies in the early mornings for Horn & Hardart's on 69th Street in Philadelphia. At night, Ed attended accounting and business law classes at the University of Pennsylvania.

At age 18, Ed and his high school friend Paul signed up as six-month reservists in the Marine Corps. After qualifying as a combat infantry rifleman in specialized infantry training, Ed volunteered to reenlist for an additional two years and awaited his deployment to Vietnam.

At that time in 1965, it was believed that the Marines would likely be the only ground troops sent to Vietnam.

Before shipping out from San Francisco, Ed played pool with Jackie Gleason at a bar, which was a memorable send-off.

He and the other Marines boarded Flying Tiger Airlines for their commercial flight to Okinawa. Ed recalls the stewardesses—pretty Korean women whom he had never seen up close before.

From Okinawa, Ed, a few dozen other Marines, and some tanks and other ground equipment traveled via a C-130 cargo plane to Đà Nẵng. At that time, the Đà Nẵng base was relatively new and small, with only Marines in residence (Army troops came later). When Ed's transport landed and the ramp lowered at the rear of the plane to release the troops and equipment, a wave of intense heat engulfed them. Ed said it felt like they had flown into an oven, something he will always remember. It was March 1966.

During the Vietnam War, a Marine infantry rifle company consisted of a headquarters section and three platoons. Each platoon consisted of three squads. Twelve to 14 Marines made up a squad, and each squad was further divided into three fire teams, each with a team leader and three other Marines.

Ed was assigned to the infantry platoon of Headquarters Company, III Marine Amphibious Force. Everyone performed a specific role, including one mortarman, one machine gunner, and one second gunner (who carried ammo). The rest were riflemen, including Ed. Everyone had to learn to shoot the machine gun. When you are one of the scrubs, you just follow orders.

Sometimes they secured areas, but more often they went on patrol looking for contact. At night, they set up ambushes because that's when the bad guys would move around. They'd set up Claymore mines, which have thousands of ball bearings inside and were set off electronically via trip wire. The mines were shaped like a dish, with the words "front towards enemy" printed on the back. So yeah, everyone in an infantry squad knew how to set Claymores.

In the beginning, Ed's squad patrolled around the base, and it was pretty easy. Đà Nẵng was turning into a big base surrounded by mountainous jungle, and they had the high ground. He even got to sleep in a regular tent.

But then they began going further out on patrols for up to two weeks. Everyone had to carry at least one bandolier (a cross-body ammo belt that feeds into the M60 machine gun), their rucksack of tactical gear, a backpack of personal gear, food, water, their rifle, ammo, and grenades. Walking point (first) was what nobody wanted to do, but everybody got their turn. Except for some nuts who liked it. While on patrol, they would protect their machine gunner at all costs.

They got resupplied every few days with choppers delivering ammo, food, water, and more Claymores. As a fire team leader, Ed got to know everyone in his squad and fire team very well because he was with them constantly.

When they were out farther like this, they slept in foxholes. Everyone had an entrenching tool, which is basically a folding shovel. Sometimes there were two guys to a hole, but usually everyone had their own hole because they had to spread out. In foxholes, the rain was miserable, but it usually meant no one was coming to your position. Some kept watch while others tried to sleep. They did not usually have a sleeping bag, just a poncho liner.

I asked about trenches. There were no trenches in Vietnam like in World War I, Ed explained, since there was no front line. There were no lines and no defined sides.

The radioman carried the radio on his back, and the bad guys were always trying to shoot out the radio. Without it, they could not relay enemy coordinates to air support so that artillery could engage the enemy. Sometimes a squad would accidentally give the wrong coordinates, resulting in friendly fire. So the lieutenant usually handled the calls.

Most of the combat was no more than 30-40 feet away, but they usually could not see who they were shooting at because of the dense jungle. They seldom saw a face. Often, they were just shooting so the enemy could not shoot. They could not see shit, so were just firing into the brush.

When back at the base, Ed was assigned to guard duty around the perimeter. If he saw the enemy, he would call it in.

Sometimes they moved by helicopter with a pilot and a gunner, which was called an aerial assault. If it was hot (taking fire) when they arrived at the LZ (landing zone), they would not land, but would fly about 4-5 feet off the ground and have to jump.

Ed's unit was sent to Chu Lai on TAD (temporary additional duty) for about a month as reinforcements, then transferred to Phú Bài Combat Base, performing infantry patrols in both locations.

After nine months in-country, while stationed at Phú Bài, Ed was promoted. Very soon after, he suffered a leg injury from VC grenade shrapnel.

The field hospital could not handle the injury, so he was sent to the Philippines, then to Yokosuka Naval Hospital in Japan for three months of treatment.

For the remainder of his recuperation, Ed was sent to the Philadelphia Naval Hospital. He met Frances Porreca, his future wife (and my mom), at a Holy Cross Catholic church dance. They slow danced, and he used a cane. They were married in November of 1967. A month later he was discharged from the service. He had been in the Marines for almost three years.

Ed is a 100% disabled veteran whose diagnoses include PTSD, scars, bilateral hearing loss, and tinnitus. He has prostate cancer (an Agent Orange presumptive), and has also suffered from various episodes of melanoma.

Ed and Fran settled in Glassboro, New Jersey, where he worked at the Owens-Illinois manufacturing plant as a lithographic machine operator until 1995. Ed then turned his creative talents towards roles as a freelance photographer and magazine writer while paying the bills as a real estate investor and property manager. He later spent about three years selling high-end fishing boats while enjoying a rock-star expense account. The economic crash of '08 put a stop to that, and retirement started to look good.

Since retiring, Ed has enjoyed travel photography and organizing small trips for both civilians and veterans, including trips to Normandy, France, and this trip to Vietnam. Fran, who also accompanied us on the trip, is a retired university finance bookkeeper and classroom scheduler. The couple has two adult children, three grandchildren, and loves to travel and spend time in their beautifully landscaped yard and pool in Sewell, Mantua Township, New Jersey.

Ed says he wants to see what the areas he fought in look like without a war going on. He is not worried about being in any of the places. He already has flashbacks, has had them for decades, reliving things that are unpleasant. He's used to it.

Mary Zelanis-Laughlin (Vietnam-era veteran)

Mary was born and raised in Paterson, New Jersey, and graduated from Paterson Central High School in 1964. She went on to graduate with a B.A. in biology from the University of Louisville, where she also attended dental school as one of only two women in a class of 50. While in college, Mary and her female classmates were often invited to USO dances. Later, Mary volunteered for the USO herself, helping to provide Saturday night dances and light Sunday lunches for the troops.

Mary graduated with her dental degree and obtained licenses in Kentucky and New Jersey in 1971. That September, she joined the Army, serving as a pioneering female dentist. At the time, male students were getting drafted into the War, and Mary joined with a sense of duty and also a desire to travel, having just completed seven years of school. Although she hoped for an assignment at the medical corps in Fort Sam Houston, Texas, Mary was destined for Fort Dix, just 80 miles from her childhood home. Mary said she joined the Army to see the world, and was sent right back to New Jersey.

Fortunately, Mary did not face discrimination due to her gender, but received only too-large or improper uniforms designed for male dentists or female nurses.

But as the only woman in her role on active duty, Mary received a lot of attention, including being featured in *The New York Times*, *The National Enquirer*, and several local newspapers. Mary joked that so many photos were taken of her that she probably had her arm around more men than most women do in a lifetime. She was also a mystery guest on the Emmy-award winning television game show *What's My Line?* Panelists on the show had to determine Mary's occupation by asking her yes or no questions. Comedic actor Soupy

Sales guessed Mary was a drill sergeant. That was the end of the guessing, and Garry Moore flipped over all of the cards.

Mary spent two years at Fort Dix, where she met her future husband, Kevin Laughlin. She treated the dental conditions of soldiers returning from Vietnam and new volunteers, as enlistment was up due to the bad economy.

After Mary's Army stint ended, she and Kevin married in 1974 and settled in Vineland, New Jersey, where she worked for the state as a staff dentist for the Vineland Developmental Center School treating severely disabled adults. Mary remained in the position for 25 years.

Wishing to have children but faced with an endometriosis diagnosis and unsuccessful in vitro attempts, she and Kevin decided to adopt. Not ones to do anything small, they adopted eight children between 1980 and 1981, four from the United States and four from Colombia, all between the ages of three and four. Years later, when the first set of children were teenagers, the couple adopted four more young children from Russia, where Kevin had been involved in a teacher's exchange program.

After 25 years in a state job, Mary worked for a private prison system in Bridgeton, New Jersey. In 2002, she joined the Coast Guard as a private contractor for eight years (but was treated as military personnel due to her veteran status). In 2010, Mary began pulling teeth and making dentures for the company Affordable Dentures in Audubon, New Jersey.

At age 78, Mary remains dedicated to her profession, working a total of 35 hours per week at Affordable Dentures, Vineland Dental, and Ancora Psychiatric Hospital.

Mary decided to join our trip for multiple reasons, primarily to support Kevin and monitor his physical and mental health, as Kevin still experiences nightmares about his service. Mary was also curious about the state of Vietnam today and planned to visit some local dental clinics.

The following section is derived from interviews with two veterans whom my dad knows from group therapy. They were unable to join our trip, but were very supportive of our endeavor. Dad and I agreed that their experiences and perspectives would help enhance the reader's understanding of the Vietnam War veteran experience.

Mike Rans

Mike was born and raised in Philadelphia and graduated from Roman Catholic High School in 1965. He joined the Navy in July of 1966 after working part-time at Children's Heart Hospital rehab facility and at Owen's Corning fiberglass factory.

Mike was assigned to the Hospital Corps after it was discovered that he had prior hospital experience. A corpsman is similar to an Army medic, providing medical care to troops. Mike completed his training at Camp Lejeune Field Medical School and New York Naval Hospital before leaving for his tour in Vietnam just before Christmas of 1967.

Mike was stationed with the 1st Battalion, 4th Marines, First Marine Division in the I Corps Tactical Zone based in Đông Hà. I Corps was the designation for the five northernmost provinces of South Vietnam during the War. As a corpsman in this region, Mike was embedded with Marines, acting as the primary medical personnel in intense combat zones that included jungle, mountains, and the DMZ.

Although technically a Navy "sailor," Marines considered a corpsman "one of us," as they went on missions together and saved the lives of countless Marines.

My dad said, for a Marine in the infantry, there is no better friend than a corpsman, because he will do anything for you.

In addition to dealing with the trauma of the wounded, corpsmen were subjected to most other facets of combat. Each platoon included one or two corpsmen, who carried only .45 automatic pistols. These "combat medics" would engage the enemy along with the rest of the platoon until someone required medical attention. Corpsmen would often move through heavy fire to reach the wounded in order to provide immediate, often life-saving care.

Along with treating combat injuries, corpsmen handled the general medical needs of their platoon, worked in hospitals, and provided medical assistance to the local Vietnamese civilian population.

After a short time at Đông Hà, Mike was in the field during Operation Kentucky, on or around Christmas Eve. After cleaning a head wound for a Marine who then walked away, Mike found himself on the ground. It was a mortar attack, and after some time, Mike realized the mortar had sent shrapnel into his neck. The injury earned him his first Purple Heart.

In January, Mike was sent to C-2 (Charlie Two) Base, part of Leatherneck Square just south of Cồn Tiên, as part of the H&S (Hospital and Supply) Company, 1st Battalion, 4th Marines. Mike remained there for about six weeks before his entire company was moved to the main base at Cồn Tiên. It was a site of fierce shelling during the War, and a place we visited during our return tour. During his time, Mike said bunkers were made of thick wooden frames reinforced with sand bags.

Mike will always remember the "mad minutes" while on patrol. This was a period of intense, concentrated weapons fire by the platoon, usually around the perimeter, but sometimes in the general area of a suspected enemy. This maximum burst of firepower was a tactic used to gain the upper hand and control potential threats. It was effective in deterring enemy attacks, discouraging infiltrators into the perimeter, and suppressing ambushes. Although the tactic predates the War, the term "mad minute" was coined in Vietnam and remains part of military vocabulary to this day.

For Mike, the most frightening part of the War was the sounds. He recalled being on patrol with Bravo Company and hearing something like a train falling out of the sky. Someone said it was probably a B-52 bomb that had gone of course.

Mike continued to recall the terror of the B-52 bombings. Sometimes, he said, when they would bomb along the DMZ, you could see the dirt flying up before you'd hear the reverberation. This could be from miles away. A few hours later, you'd feel the artillery response cracking on the ground. It was chilling, Mike said.

But overall, Mike did not have a horrible time at Cồn Tiên, because after a while they got into a routine. They would get shelled every day at 5:10 or 5:15 p.m. for about 10-15 minutes. Sometimes it was artillery, sometimes rocket fire. Artillery was shot from far away, from a big gun on wheels. Rockets were the largest shells and were launched. Mike said it was meant to be harassment, and the Marines called it "shelling with your dinner."

Some of the Marines created their own routine at Cồn Tiên: they caught rats. Mike caught 31 rats in 31 days. Sometimes you could feel them running over you when you tried to sleep.

Mike remained at Cồn Tiên for about two months, then was transferred to Bravo Company, dug in just to the west of Cồn Tiên.

On May 22, 1968, 17 Marines, including the lieutenant and captain, were killed after being ambushed by a large group of NVA. During the battle, Mike was shot in the leg by enemy fire while crawling through the grass to a wounded Marine. Luckily, he was wearing a flak jacket (a type of body armor), which may have saved his life.

Mike was treated at multiple facilities before ending up at Yokosuka Naval Hospital in Japan for about a month. He received skin grafts as part of his treatment and was awarded a second Purple Heart. On July 4, 1968, he flew home to the Philadelphia Naval Hospital, where he worked until the end of his tour on April 27, 1970. He held various roles, including security, funeral escort, and performing patient testing in the gastroenterology department.

After his service ended, Mike earned his nursing degree, then took a job at the Children's Hospital of Philadelphia (CHOP). There, he met his future wife Sue, also a nurse. The couple married in August 1975 and soon after moved to New Jersey. They have two children and two grandchildren.Mike worked as a nurse at CHOP for 43 years before retiring in 2014.

The VA has designated Mike as an 80% disabled veteran with unemployability, consisting of a 50% rating for PTSD and 30% for type 2 diabetes (an Agent Orange presumptive).

Mike told me about the Angel Fire Vietnam Veterans Memorial in New Mexico. The memorial is dedicated to all Vietnam veterans who sacrificed their lives in the War and specifically honors the 17 Marines who died at Cồn Tiên on May 22, 1968, during the ambush in which Mike's leg was wounded. Created by Dr. Victor Westphall, whose son, David, was the lieutenant who lost his life there, Angel Fire was the first major Vietnam War memorial in the United States. Mike urges anyone in the area to visit.

During the War, the dangerous role of the corpsman resulted in high fatality rates. While approximately 10,000 served, 645 corpsmen were killed, and over 3,300 were wounded. That's a death rate of 6.45%, higher than the overall Marine Corps death rate of 5.0%, the highest of all military branches.

Though perilous, the role of the corpsman in Vietnam was essential to Marines achieving an exceptionally high survival rate of 96-98% for those wounded in action. Many Marines returned home thanks to their corpsman's ability to provide immediate care during combat and the swift arrival of "Dustoff" medevac evacuation helicopters. Named for the clouds of dust kicked up during landings and takeoffs, Dustoff crews flew unarmed Huey helicopters into dangerous "hot" zones to extract the wounded while continuing life-saving care en route to the hospital.

Four Navy corpsmen earned the Medal of Honor for their valor in Vietnam. To date, the Hospital Corps remains the most decorated rate (job) in the U.S. military.

Enrico (Rick) Storino

Rick was born in Italy and grew up in Northeast Philadelphia. After graduating from high school, he worked at the family butcher shop. When he was drafted to go to Vietnam in 1970, he challenged the notice since he held a green card and was not a U.S. citizen. He was told that he was technically correct, but that he'd be deported if he didn't go to war. His whole family was in the United States at this point, and he didn't really know anyone in Italy. He decided to take his chances.

Rick attended basic training at Fort Bragg, North Carolina, then was assigned the Military occupational specialty (MOS) of baker/cook, due to his background in the meat industry. He attended Quartermaster Corps school at Fort Lee, Virginia, for training.

In the summer of 1971, Rick was assigned as a cook and stationed at Landing Zone Hawk Hill near Chữ Lãi in Central Vietnam as part of the 196th Light Infantry Brigade (the "Chargers"). There was no established base there, with fewer than 100 soldiers stationed at the site. They lived in underground bunkers, essentially large foxholes, dug by the Army Corps of Engineers.

The zone took a lot of incoming fire, and when a concussion bomb struck, Rick was knocked unconscious and thrown up a ramp. He lost his hearing for a while, but remarkably, didn't get a scratch on him. On another occasion, a Vietnamese civilian entered the mess hall with a satchel charge around her neck and blew herself up, taking out a bunch of people with her.

Rick is small in stature, and one day a head honcho came into the mess hall and told him they were looking for tunnel rat volunteers. These intrepid soldiers were the unsung heroes of the War, conducting perilous underground missions against the Việt Cộng in extremely dangerous conditions.

When the Army asks for volunteers, there's really no choice in the matter, so Rick reluctantly accepted. Although he never re-

ceived tunnel-rat training, he was transferred to the 198th Light Infantry Brigade out of Củ Chi. Soldiers who had formal training knew what they were doing, but some, like Rick, had to learn on the job. Luckily, Rick had a platoon leader who took him under his wing.

If there was a lot of activity in an area, there was probably an active tunnel below. Experienced E-6s (equivalent to staff sergeants) had the odious job of finding trap doors to the tunnels, and Rick felt that the Army treated these guys as expendable. The entrances were small, well-hidden, and hard to find. Since the enemy was accustomed to living in the tunnels, Rick said that sometimes they could smell them out.

More tunnel holes were found in villages than out in the jungle, Rick explained. Some locals gave away enemy locations or entrances, while others hid the enemy. The Việt Cộng often coerced or threatened villagers to cooperate. Sometimes you were sure they were friendly, but you turned out to be wrong. Barbers and other locals who worked on the base would listen to soldiers talking and relay info to the enemy. Six out of their nine barbers were caught on the barbed wire one night trying to sabotage Rick's base. They probably cut his hair, and he may have faced them in a tunnel.

Even the ARVN could not be trusted, Rick said. When things got rough, they'd disappear, and sometimes they'd fight against you at night.

Rick was scared the first time he entered a tunnel, but was thankful that he never got claustrophobic. Those who did would yell and scream, and they would be immediately taken out and moved off the assignment. If you made it the third time without an "episode," Rick recalled, they'd say, "you're in heaven."

The tunnel rats always went on missions in groups of three. The first two were tied together no more than eight feet apart before crawling in, while the third stayed topside to keep watch. This process was rotated each mission. When the entrances were vertical, they were lowered in a basket or chair down into the holes.

When the missions began, rats went down with a pistol, headlamp, and knife. But when people started getting shot due to the headlamps giving them away, they were given handheld flashlights. Rick eventually abandoned his light entirely out of distrust. Everything was subject to a booby trap, even their gear.

Because the Việt Cộng stayed underground during the day, the rats typically entered in daylight, forcing their eyes to adjust slowly to the pitch black.

Descending was a slow process. It raised your anxiety, but it made you more aware, Rick explained.

Once inside, Rick said your arms were always extended to check for trip wires, and you would feel the wall for indentations.

In addition to booby traps, the soldiers faced poisonous snakes, insects, and sometimes unstable tunnels.

The stench was horrible because the Việt Cộng would relieve themselves in the tunnels, and sometimes leave their dead to rot. They would carve out an indentation and stick the corpse in the wall. Consequently, tunnels rats endured the waking nightmare of touching decomposing bodies as they navigated the darkness. Unlike their enemy, Rick said he and the other rats never left their dead behind.

While a common myth suggested that Americans dropped grenades into the tunnels, Rick explained this was rare because the tunnels had a lot of twists and turns. The Việt Cộng—both men and women—would try to stab you as you were coming around the corner.

The missions varied. Sometimes his team would be assigned to get documents, sometimes to clear tunnels or destroy supplies. If you engaged the enemy, Rick said, all hell would break loose. If you saw anything move, you fired only one shot at a time. Firing more than three was a distress signal to the surface. While rats were issued a .45 pistol, most carried a personal backup. Rick's weapon of choice was a 9mm Beretta.

Rick said that when you came up into the sunlight, your mind was racing, and it took some time to come down from that.

Although the teams of three were rotated so you couldn't get too close to anyone, Rick says they were all part of a larger group with different methods of looking out for each other. He feels lucky to have been part of that group.

Rick served as a tunnel rat for about four months before becoming an 11 Bravo infantry rifleman. His time in the tunnels earned him an early release and a Bronze Star. Although some served in tunnels their entire tour, tunnel rat duty was often limited due to the intense psychological toll and high casualty rate.

When he came home in 1972, Rick felt like he was just floating along, and he had trouble holding jobs. He never opened up to his parents about his time as a rat, telling them he only worked as a cook. Rick did not tell anyone because he wanted to forget the experience and certainly did not want to relive it by talking about it. He has never discussed these experiences with his wife and kids, either, only other veterans. I feel honored that Rick decided to tell his story for this book.

In 2012, Rick was classified as 100% disabled: 90% for PTSD and 10% for ischemic heart disease, for which he underwent a triple bypass.

Rick sees a psychologist once a month. Sometimes he still can't go into a dark room. Sometimes he still reaches for switches so he can turn on the lights before entering.

Part Two

The Campaign

Festive décor celebrating the city's cultural and artistic heritage is featured on many of Hà Nội's buildings.

The world is a book and those who do not travel read only one page.

—St. Augustine

Seasoned travelers understand that it's not only the highlights, but also the sum of the small and seemingly insignificant anecdotes that make up a place. It's the insightful smile from a restaurant server, the unfamiliar way sunlight reflects off a city skyline, the exotic smells of a marketplace, and the unique handicrafts of a proud craftswoman that blend into the tale of your experience. Rather than chronicling everything we saw or experienced in each city, village, museum, temple, restaurant, or roadside stand, I will instead attempt to give you a taste of the more significant, profound, and unexpected adventures our group and I experienced. By providing detailed descriptions, comparisons, and personal reflections, I hope to also give you a broad sketch of what it was like to be there. This approach should convey not only a sense of the veterans' visit to a place that helped define them, but also a glimpse into the nature of this fascinating country, so compellingly different from our own.

After two preparation meetings to discuss itineraries, getting our visas sorted, and enduring long, tedious phone calls with the airline to ensure we were seated with spouses or family members, we were finally set for our trip. In April 2023, our group of 10 travelers, including six veterans, was eager to take off.

I'm used to international travel, so the packing and other trip preparations were no big deal. It was the air travel I dreaded: a 12-hour flight to Doha, a 14-hour layover, and another eight-hour flight to Hà Nội. I had to mentally prepare myself for my hopeful Zen time in a metal tube of recycled air, especially in the confines of coach class.

With a little help from Xanax and bourbon, I reached the serenity required to get through the flights and layover. We flew Qatar Airways, and the plane, service, and food were all excellent;

I would definitely choose them again if given the opportunity. Our group even took in a four-hour city tour of Doha during the layover, which was an added bonus and gave me a small taste of the Middle East, leaving me hoping for a bigger bite in the future.

After what seemed like an eternity (and was, regarding air travel, as Vietnam is literally halfway around the world from the east coast of the United States), we arrived in Hà Nội. Our guide, Thế (pronounced Tay), collected our weary group at the airport with a cardboard sign and an insistence on loading each piece of luggage. Having someone else take charge of every detail was a welcome change from trying to keep ourselves alert and mobile in our zombie-like states.

The North

A Capital City

We were deposited in a posh boutique hotel in the old section of Hà Nội. The modernist serenity of our air-conditioned base offered a sharp contrast to the steamy, vibrant, and bustling streets just outside the door.

Many produce sellers in Hà Nội transport their goods by bicycle.

Shops and vendors stay open late in Hà Nội's Old Quarter.

Hà Nội is an ancient yet thriving city with a dual nature. Tree-lined boulevards with towering skyscrapers intersect narrow alleys jammed with overflowing shops and eateries, with historical sites scattered throughout. As anyone who has visited a city in Vietnam can tell you, the motorbikes are everywhere, more plentiful than cars and operated by seemingly fearless locals of all ages and economic status. The only rule of the road seems to be don't get hit or hit anyone. Although we did not witness any, accidents occur, of course, but not nearly at the rate one would expect based on operator behavior. The number of motorbikes weaving among each other, through eight-lane intersections of heavy, fast-moving traffic, cutting in front of large buses and trucks, and piled with extraordinary amounts of cargo—including entire families—was unreal.

Somehow, in that chaos, was a synchronicity beyond established reason. The fluid and seamless way vehicles flowed along every congested roadway we traveled in Vietnam is an unexplained phenomenon akin to aliens, ghosts, and other paranormal activities: one has to experience it to believe it.

The Huc Bridge, also known as the "Rising Sun Bridge," is a vibrant red, wooden bridge that connects the shore to Jade Islet in Hà Nội.

Vietnam is the third-largest exporter of textiles in the world, behind China and Bangladesh.

Hà Nội's pedestrians are dealt a sensory smorgasbord. Food is for sale in all its forms—prepared and ready to eat, just butchered and raw, or still swimming, hopping, or clucking. Produce is remarkably fresh, varied, and inexpensive, available at stands or off the backs of precariously-balanced bicycles. Alleyways teem with enough traditional dresses, custom-made suits, bawdy t-shirts, designer jeans, sensible footwear, and novelty socks to wardrobe the planet. The call of sellers inviting each passer-by to examine the

Saint Joseph's Cathedral, the oldest Catholic church in Hà Nội, was built in 1886.

Street musicians often perform traditional music in Hà Nội.

goods reverberates off the buildings to form a cacophony of capitalism in this supposedly socialist stronghold.

Elaborate personal shrines at entryways to homes and businesses are common—small to medium box-like structures with gold and red curlicued tops and sides. Items inside vary, including photos of deceased loved ones, deity idols, glowing electric candles, tropical blossoms, real or fake money, over-ripe fruit, packaged snacks, and cups of tea. The abundance of burning incense permeates the streets, and its pungent smoke tickled my nasal cilia.

While most of our group retired early that first night, my dad and I decided to explore the neighborhood around the hotel, including the famous "Beer Street," a swarming plethora of imbibing youth hopping from one small stall to the next. My dad insisted on "fresh" beer, what they call draught in that part of the country, and we dodged pockets of festive twenty-somethings until we found the perfect stall to enjoy some local brew, which set us back about a dollar for two glasses. We people-watched a mingling blend of Asian and Anglo (mostly Australian) kids shuffle by as we were serenaded by battling techno music from multiple angles. One surprising reality throughout Vietnam is that most casual outdoor establishments seat everyone—locals and tourists alike—in mini plastic kiddie chairs, and Dad and I plunked down in pink unicorn seats to sip our brew. It's one thing if you're a small-statured Asian person, but another if you're a six-foot Anglo-American trying to pile yourself onto the wobbly little lightweight base, as many of our group had to do. This peculiarity gave us a few hearty chuckles during our visit.

Hỏa Lò Prison (Hanoi Hilton)

Our first group excursion in Hà Nội began with the famous Hỏa Lò Prison, known to most Americans as the "Hanoi Hilton." The structure, a seemingly benevolent golden-yellow relic sitting in the middle of a bustling neighborhood, was built by the French beginning in 1886, when Vietnam was still part of French Indochina. During the Vietnam War, it housed mostly American pilots shot down during bombing raids, and was known for torturing prisoners and holding them in unsanitary and inhumane conditions. Much of the original structure has been taken down to make room for development, including the area that housed American prisoners during the War, while the gatehouse section that remains has become a museum.

French colonists first used the complex to imprison, interrogate, and torture communist dissidents who sought independence, including a large number of women inmates. In the section currently dedicated to the French era, there is an authentic, somber display of windowless cement cells (with "beds" of cement blocks), chains, torture devices, and photographs of the barbaric conditions. There's also an original guillotine on display, and seeing this device firsthand was a chilling testament to the savagery inflicted on the political prisoners held here.

While the museum bestows the title of national heroes upon the communist dissidents, the American War section of the museum conveys a different sentiment. As an American, it can be mildly shocking to see your country's war heroes and POWs referred to as enemies and conspirators, quickly reminding you that you're in a different country with a very different history and culture. Some photos include captions claiming that American prisoners were

One of the original entrance gates to Hỏa Lò Prison, also known as "Hanoi Hilton," is shown here. The prison was built and used by the French colonists to hold political prisoners, then used by North Vietnam to hold U.S. Prisoners of War, and lastly used to incarcerate Vietnamese dissidents until its demolition between 1993 and 1994.

A photo display at the Hỏa Lò prison museum features the release of American POWs on March 14, 1973. The man in the first row at right is Senator John S. McCain, who was a Navy pilot at the time. One-hundred and eight U.S. service members were released on that day.

Our guide speaks to three of our veterans at the Hỏa Lò prison complex. The visit revealed some uncomfortable truths to our veterans.

A photo display at the Hỏa Lò prison museum shows Hà Nội Knitting factory workers firing a 50-caliber machine gun during a training session in 1972.

treated humanely and fairly, a claim still officially held by the Vietnamese government, yet a view certainly not shared by American prisoner accounts. As Winston Churchill said, "History is written by the victors," and as a Western visitor to Vietnam, that quote becomes a firsthand lesson.

Although the American soldiers were labeled as enemies in all War-era photographic displays, as we approached the end of the exhibit, we viewed photos of John McCain and other former American pilots returning decades later, shaking hands with their former enemies, all now considered "friends and brothers" by the Vietnamese. The message seemed to be that the Americans were our arch-nemeses then, but now we are friends, a position that seemed to resonate everywhere we visited.

While the offer of the hand of friendship was certainly appreciated, the irony was not lost on me at Hỏa Lò. The communist dissidents who were tortured by the French were considered heroes, with a large number of tangible items and photos to prove what they endured. This use of torture was descriptive and highly condemned. But by all American accounts, the Vietnamese communists, whose forbearers were tortured on this same spot, tortured our pilots. As an American who knows this truth, it makes me think . . . did these people not learn? Torture is fine as long as it's done to the right people? I'm not naïve, but doesn't it look ridiculous to condemn torture and claim there was no torture of Americans, when every American visitor who understands a shred of our history knows otherwise? Don't get me wrong—I am aware that some in our own military committed treacherous acts during the War. Yet it's been decades since these acts have been acknowledged and overwhelmingly condemned as the horrific war crimes that they were. This awareness made the blatant denial of the reality within Hỏa Lò disconcerting, and I think the visit left our group, especially the veterans, a bit rattled.

Uncle Hồ

A must-see in Hà Nội is the imposing mausoleum and tomb of Hồ Chí Minh, Chairman of the Workers' Party of Vietnam from 1951 until his death in 1969. Vietnamese citizens laud "Uncle" Hồ as the father of the Democratic Republic of Vietnam and founder

The mausoleum of revolutionary leader Hồ Chí Minh is located in Hà Nội's Ba Đình Square, where he declared Vietnam's independence in 1945. The imposing granite structure is modeled after Lenin's mausoleum in Moscow, yet incorporates distinct Vietnamese design elements.

of its Communist Party, and many make pilgrimages from remote villages to view their beloved leader. Hồ Chí Minh is often referred to as "Uncle Hồ" because he was viewed by his countrymen as a benevolent, paternal figure and a humble patriot who dedicated his life to Vietnamese independence. This affectionate nickname also reflects his populist appeal, stemming from his simple lifestyle and regular visits to villages and schools where he would interact directly with children.

The site requires visitors to observe strict rules of reverence and heed the abundant and watchful armed military guards. Even while approaching the mausoleum grounds, cameras, phones, revealing attire, talking, food, drink, congregating, or stopping are not permitted. I also discovered that questions are sorely frowned upon.

After traversing a labyrinth of roped pathways, each caller eventually reaches the mecca of their visit: the icy cold tomb room (and the best air-conditioning in Vietnam, I would venture). When crossing the dimly-lit, red-carpeted chamber to view Hồ's embalmed corpse, visitors shuffle through one-by-one and cannot linger more than a few seconds. The esteemed uncle appears to be merely asleep in his untouchable glass case. It's a deathly silent, eerily formal

Behind the mausoleum sits the Hồ Chí Minh Museum, inaugurated in 1990 to commemorate the President's 100th birthday. It houses a vast collection that chronicles the leader's personal journey and pivotal role in Vietnam's struggle for independence.

experience for a Westerner, and although I am thankful to have gotten a glimpse of the famous man's remains, I was relieved to exit the mausoleum and remove myself from the suspicious scrutiny of the guards. As our group went through the line, they seemed to be anticipating one of us to make a fatal slip-up (or maybe I was just being paranoid).

Sacred Places

Near the Hồ Chí Minh Mausoleum sits the One Pillar Pagoda. First built in 1049 of wood and a single stone pillar, the structure is shaped like a lotus, the national flower of Vietnam. Behind the

The One Pillar Pagoda in Hà Nội is so named because it is built on only one pillar, called the Liên Hoa Đài, or "the lotus pedestal." In Buddhist tradition, the lotus flower symbolizes purity and spiritual awakening, as its magnificent flowers blossom in murky waters to rise above the "mud" of suffering and desire.

pagoda grows a ficus tree, believed to be one of the offshoots of the famous bodhi tree under which the Buddha Siddhartha Gautama attained enlightenment. Visitors await their turn to climb the small temple's steps to peer at the colorful shrine dedicated to the popular

The Temple of Literature, or Văn Miếu, was first constructed in 1070 during the Trần Dynasty, with major restorations taking place in 1920, 1954, and 2000. Despite wars and natural disasters, the temple has preserved ancient architectural styles and relics of many dynasties.

female bodhisattva Quan Âm. In Buddhist tradition, a bodhisattva forgoes or delays enlightenment to help ease the suffering of others.

Another notable stop in Hà Nội was Quốc Tử Giám, or the Temple of Literature, an historical relic, active temple, and home to

An altar featuring a statue of Confucius stands inside Hà Nội's Temple of Literature. One tenet of its philosophy emphasizes virtue and morality in government. Confucius opined that a leader who governs by virtue is like the North Star, remaining in place while all other stars revolve around it.

Vietnam's first national university. The complex was built in 1070 and celebrates the Chinese philosopher Confucius (551-479 BCE) and the scholarly pursuits of knowledge and wisdom. The site is

The stone "Doctor's Stelae" in the Temple of Literature honors academics who passed the rigorous imperial examinations held between 1442 and 1779. Each tablet rests on a stone tortoise base, symbolizing longevity and wisdom.

Our guide, Thế, speaks to us before we enter the Trấn Quốc Pagoda, the oldest Buddhist temple in Hà Nội. It was originally built in the 6th century on the banks of the Red River and moved to its current location on Golden Fish Island in 1615.

made up of multiple courtyards, formal gardens, and buildings with ornate altar rooms. Plentiful offerings surround imposing idols of the renowned philosopher and his disciples.

Although sometimes hard to define, Confucianism is generally considered a way of life focusing on individual ethics and morality with a slant towards humanism, ancestor respect, and rational thought. Over the more than twenty-five hundred years since its inception, Confucianism has resurfaced and evolved many times, but its ethos still holds universal truth and value in many cultures. Examined in depth, Confucianism can reveal a beautiful, stark simplicity when all the bells and whistles of any accompanying religious dogma are removed.

Our group also visited the impressive Trấn Quốc Pagoda and complex, which is at least 1,500 years old and the oldest in Hà Nội. Monks still live on the grounds, which include multiple buildings,

The Trấn Quốc Pagoda's famous 11-story Lotus Stupa features a white Amitabha Buddha statue in each of the tier's six archways, and is crowned with a nine-layered gemstone lotus, symbolizing spiritual ascension.

The three "Mẫu" or "Mothers," are housed inside a shrine at the Trấn Quốc Pagoda Complex. The goddesses are central figures in the Vietnamese folk religion of Đạo Mẫu, a belief system which honors female deities and spirits who govern various realms of the universe.

gardens, and another descendant of the famed bodhi tree. One of the shrines houses famous statues of the three "Mẫu" or "Mothers." The green mother has domain over the mountains and forests, the white over the water, and the red over the sky. These indigenous goddesses predate Buddhism and are some of the oldest deities in Vietnam.

The Quan Thanh Taoist temple, with its animal symbolism and famous black bronze statue of the deity Trấn Vũ, concluded our northern tour of revered places. Taoism can be briefly summarized as a religious philosophy that emphasizes living in harmony with all aspects of nature and the Universe, and many elements of it have been absorbed into Vietnamese folk religions.

Visiting these sacred sites was not only interesting from an historical and architectural standpoint, but it also helped us gain a better understanding of Vietnam's inhabitants. Tenets of Buddhism, Taoism, and Confucianism often overlap with the more common folk religions that emphasize ancestor veneration, and all are ingrained in the culture and identity of the Vietnamese people. Although many—especially the young—tend to be irreligious, the temperament and psyche of many residents seem to reflect the overarching philosophies of these beliefs.

Colleen and Fran with our guide, Thế, in front of the Lotus Stupa.

Pilgrims circumnavigate the Trấn Quốc Pagoda Complex's Bodhi tree offshoot, reportedly a cutting from the original tree in India where Buddha Siddhartha attained enlightenment. The tree is circled to honor its religious significance or to make wishes and seek blessings.

Masters of Puppets

Another cultural immersion we experienced was a water puppet show, an ancient North Vietnamese art form dating from the 11th century. Elaborate puppets glide across a wide, shallow pool, accompanied by live musical and vocal performances. There's no dialogue, yet the international audience giggles in unison with the characters' shenanigans. This fanciful ambiance, combined with a

Water puppetry audiences are treated to a visual and olfactory feast. Bamboo rods support puppets that glide through a waist-deep pool, a custom derived from 11th-century village performances in the Red River Delta's flooded rice fields.

stunningly vivid set design and rhythmic lighting, made me feel as if I were floating in a childlike, utopian dreamland.

Ninh Bình

While in the north, our group traveled by bus to the Red River Delta in the Province of Ninh Bình, about 90 kilometers south of Hà Nội. We began by walking through the ancient city of Hoa Lư and its King Đinh Temple at the foot of Ma Yên Mountain, seat of the country's first capital. We then boarded multiple bamboo "sampans," each piloted by a stealthy oarswoman who alternately used her hands and feet to power us along the Ngô Đồng River. The weather was wet and misty, adding to the surreal voyage along waterways meandering between towering bluffs. We were silent travelers, with the only sounds being the pull of an oar through water or the occasional click of a photograph.

Traversing this famous karst region—jagged limestone cliffs encompassing underground streams and caverns—I was surprised

Colleen stands on a scenic bridge in the ancient complex of Hoa Lư, Vietnam's first capital.

A Chinese-style guardian lion, also called a foo dog, overlooks the mountains and forests.

Ed and his wife Fran are ready to embark on a misty sampan tour of the Tràng An Landscape Complex.

Our veteran travelers enjoy the lush green scenery along the Ngô Đồng River.

Several pagodas and temples line the shore, used for Buddhist worship, prayer and meditation, cultural and historical reflection, and retreats.

Our tour took us through caverns under the limestone cliffs. The complex's caves hold the historical significance of providing shelter to humans for over 30,000 years. This rich archaeological record is revealed by the evidence of tools, burial sites, and cooking remains, suggesting long-term habitation and adaptation to the environment.

to glimpse several fog-draped family shrines and temples along the shoreline. Even in this remote setting, among narrow banks and soaring escarpments, were the requisite ancestral sanctums. My artist's eye savored how the intricate pagoda roofing and red-and-gold-hued sarcophagi created a striking contrast to the surrounding vegetation, all crowned by silvery escarpments that graduated into a soft sky.

Our journey continued through caverns, and I touched their craggy, cool walls as we glided along. I inhaled deeply, letting the sweet and vegetal, oxygen-rich mist inflate my lungs. Tràng An is a World Heritage Site, with not only "post-card-perfect" views, but an experience that rewards all the senses. The encounter left me with a peaceful serenity that lingered for several days.

Pearls and Peonies

Our northern tour continued with an educational visit to a pearl farm, factory, and showroom where the famous Hạ Long Bay saltwater pearls are cultivated and crafted into jewelry. I splurged

Although a popular tourist destination, Hạ Long Bay is also home to those who live and work on the water.

Hạ Long Bay is famous for its cultured saltwater pearls. Large-scale operations use Japanese technology to implant nuclei in oysters for consistent, high-purity pearls of multiple colors.

Our first glimpse of the stunning Hạ Long Bay limestone karsts. Hạ Long fittingly translates as "descending dragon."

and treated myself to a pair of lovely black pearl drop earrings set in silver.

Next, we enjoyed a two-day stay on the small Peony Cruise line through Hạ Long Bay, part of the South China Sea. The ship was luxurious and well-appointed, with tuxedoed waitstaff, first-class dining options, and premium suites, all with private balconies. We waded in the on-deck pool, had our goose-down pillows hand-fluffed, and drank fancy cocktails garnished with carved exotic fruits. Fittingly, majestic peonies of many colors adorned our dining tables. Some of us joined the optional side trips, including a visit to Trung Tràng Cave on Cát Bà Island.

Although our trip to Vietnam centered around the veterans' re-visit to the country, this part in particular was an indulgent holiday. The scenery was stunning and otherworldly, a larger–scale version of the intimate sampan tour experienced just a few days prior. The glassy bay shimmered with reflections of the limestone behemoths that jutted skyward, unlike any mountains I had ever seen. As the

Cát Bà is the largest island comprising the Cát Bà Archipelago, and is known for its beautiful scenery and network of caves. Colleen and Agnes visited Trung Trang Cave, situated under 300 meters of dense forest and filled with dramatic formations.

Simple wooden fishing boats, also called junk boats, have been used for centuries along Hạ Long Bay. Many anglers focus on night squid fishing, using underwater lights to lure the squid into nets.

sun went down, I sipped rum and watched a lone osprey nosedive into still waters.

The next morning, as I participated in on-deck tai chi, the haze erased the horizon and melded the bay, land, and sky into a tranquil, monochromatic watercolor scene.

Last of Hà Nội

On the way to the airport before departing Hà Nội, we took a quick peek along the famous 'Train Street' (where a train travels down a narrow alley twice a day as people sip drinks beside the tracks), then visited the Thu Hương Lacquer Arts studio and showroom.

Although it seemed a bit like a tourist trap, we attended a free presentation on how traditional lacquer paintings, vases, and other handicrafts are created. Artists (who the studio guide claimed were disabled victims of intergenerational Agent Orange exposure) apply layer upon layer of traditional paint made from the resinous sap of native lacquer trees. Small bits of eggshell or abalone shell are often incorporated into the construction, a very detailed and painstaking process that employs magnifying lenses, tweezers, and other specialized tools. The result is vibrant work that reflects an ancient

Train Street in Hà Nội is a narrow thoroughfare where railcars pass through several times a day. Tracks are placed dangerously close to residential and commercial buildings, and tourists enjoy sipping drinks in the street's small cafés, hoping to witness a train go by.

Artisans create pieces at a lacquerware workshop to sell in its adjoining showroom. This national art form is known as sơn mài, with the lacquer paint made from the sap, or resin, of the lacquer tree. Materials like eggshells, abalone, and precious metals are often incorporated into the design.

It's not uncommon to see motorbike riders with immense amounts of cargo, highlighting their ingenuity and efficiency.

Hà Nội's Old Quarter offers an extensive array of prepared foods. This type of vendor, often called cơm bình dân, or "ordinary rice," allows customers to choose from a variety of family-style dishes that are heaped onto a plate of hot rice.

Many street vendors transport their wares on a traditional bamboo shoulder pole with twin baskets, called quang gánh, and don traditional conical hats, known as nón lá.

East Asian craft. I bought two small traditional seascape images. Although I saw similar pieces in a tourist shop several days later, I hoped (perhaps naïvely) that my pricier options supported the artists to a greater degree.

Produce vendors offer a huge assortment of fruits and vegetables, including the humble banana. I spotted at least six distinct varieties at many market stalls, with small street vendors such as this selling at least two varieties. Each offers a distinct color, flavor, and texture, and is used in various cooked and raw applications.

The Central Region

A Chance Encounter at The Huế Citadel

The central leg of our trip began after a short flight from Hà Nội to Huế. I anxiously anticipated the large number of war-related spots in this region, and wondered if our veterans were mentally preparing themselves to visit these places.

The city of Huế (pronounced *hWAY*) is a major cultural and historical center and home to the 19th century Đại Nội Citadel and Imperial City. Its more recent history includes the bloodiest massacre of the Vietnam War: The Battle of Huế, which occurred during the Tết Offensive in 1968.

On January 31, 1968, on orders from North Vietnamese officials, the Việt Cộng and People's Army of Vietnam (PAVN) took hold of the city. They immediately began purging non-communist forces, including government officials, political/civil servants, and their families. They went on to mass murder common civilians, including those who ran from questioning or spoke against the occupation, Catholic priests, German university professors, non-military

Ray overlooks the Imperial City of Huế.

The Ngọ Môn, or the Meridian Gate, was built in 1833 during the Nguyễn Dynasty. It was used exclusively by the emperor and is the grand southern and ceremonial entrance to the city.

U.S. officials, and anyone perceived as friendly to American forces. Most were summarily bound, tortured, and shot, while others were buried alive. In the months and years that followed, dozens of mass graves were uncovered in and around the city.

Within days of the city's capture, U.S. Marines and soldiers, along with ARVN troops, entered the city and waged a 26-day battle to wrest control from the North Vietnamese. Although they eventually declared victory, the city was virtually destroyed, leaving an estimated 2,800 to 6,000 civilians executed or missing and 668 American Marines and allied forces killed.

Due to its massive impact, the Battle of Huế helped define the American public's negative perception of the War. After the battle, some communist officials claimed that civilian death tolls were exaggerated by American and South Vietnamese propaganda. Even today, the massacre during the battle remains unrecognized in the Vietnamese communist government's War Remnants Museum in Hồ Chí Minh City.

Despite this grim account and the bombing that accompanied it, much of Huế's Imperial City within the Citadel grounds remains intact. Substantial stone walls and a moat bespeak the site's

The Emperor's reading pavilion, or Thái Bình Lâu, translates to pavilion of supreme peace, a tranquil space made of precious woods, and designed for intellectual and artistic pursuits away from the affairs of state.

The Five Phoenixes Pavilion, or Ngũ Phụng Lâu, recently underwent an eight-year restoration project. It consists of two floors and an ironwood structure supported by 100 pillars. The great drum, shown here, along with the great bell, were used to summon officials to gatherings.

importance, which acted as the capital of the feudal Nguyễn Dynasty from 1802 to 1945. Our group toured the expansive gardens, ancient tombs, and intact ruins with beautifully preserved interiors, and took a walk along the scenic Perfume River bank. For some of our veterans, that riverside stroll led to the most profound moment of the trip.

Our central regional guide was the energetic and smiling Anh-Cơ, and he kept us moving in good humor. Anh-Cơ's intricate knowledge of his country's history—especially the American War era—was impressive.

Prior to the trip, Dad had enquired about our veterans meeting former enemy combatants, but our planner was not able to secure this request, a fact of which Anh-Cơ was aware.

While casually enjoying the serene Perfume River within the Citadel grounds, we passed a group of uniformed soldiers. Anh-Cơ stopped and began an enthusiastic conversation with them, and our group gathered around to find out what all the fuss was about.

Former NVA! They are former NVA, our excited guide told us. He continued his discussion with them, letting them know that our group included American War veterans. Then, it began to become clear to all of us, as we noticed that the uniformed soldiers were older gentlemen like our vets.

They were former North Vietnamese soldiers, and any one of these individuals may have fought against any one of our veterans during the War.

It was a surreal experience, with our vets and theirs shaking hands. Some of them and some of us were a little standoffish; some of them and some of us were smiling and enthusiastic. Some of them seemed genuinely impressed with my dad's U.S. Marine status (once a Marine, always a Marine). In the end, everyone shook hands and lined up for a few group photos.

As the two sets of veterans mingled, we non-vets stood back. I watched my dad's face throughout the encounter. How would he react to meeting his former enemy?

His smile was extraordinary. The meeting he wanted took place after all, and the fact that it was a surprise, chance encounter seemed to make it all the more successful (with no pre-meeting anxiety). Watching my dad's big grin and exuberant handshakes, it was as if I was watching something slide off him. He seemed to get lighter, stand a bit taller. Was the dark demon losing some of its

The moment we first encountered the Vietnamese veterans, before any in our group realized they were former NVA enemy combatants.

Ed shakes hands with his former enemy.

A pivotal moment for Kevin.

power? Did seeing these men—former mortal enemies, but now a bunch of old grandpops like him—spark a flame of healing?

The entire meeting lasted about 10-15 minutes, but it seemed longer, or shorter, or lost somewhere in history and untimed. As the two groups went their separate ways, our vets took a moment to sit on shaded park benches.

Mom and I noticed that tears had welled up in one of our vets' eyes. He told us he was OK and just needed a minute. We left him alone to collect his thoughts. A couple of other vets walked around looking a bit stunned. Dad was still animated and excited. The emotional reactions ran the gamut.

The next night, Kevin, one of our vets and the group therapist, discussed the encounter with everyone. One vet reported that he couldn't sleep after experiencing a nightmare where the meeting ended with the former NVA soldiers pulling a gun on him. Maybe it's because they were in uniform, and maybe that's why the meeting gave me a nightmare, he theorized.

It turns out the former NVA veterans we met were at the Citadel and in uniform to celebrate the upcoming Reunification Day, marking the rejoining of North and South Vietnam.

They were commemorating a war America technically lost, a war that still leaves a deep scar on the psyche of our country, our veterans, and millions more like them. Our military never lost a major battle in that war, yet American politics led to the bitter outcome our vets will never forget.

The encounter revealed the commonality of humanity: no matter the side, all soldiers spill red blood. If they make it out alive, they can continue with their lives and grow old.

But it also revealed another truth to me: that whether we are conscious of it or not, our home country distinguishes us and, as Americans, often sets us apart. Even for those of us with the earnest belief that everyone on this Earth is part of one human family, the

Perhaps the most profound moment of our trip was when some of our veterans met their former enemies.

identity we share as Americans is something we cannot evade, even if we wanted to. Even I, a non-veteran, was more disturbed by that fact that the NVA vets were celebrating the defeat of my country than the fact that they were former enemies of the United States. I know that the Vietnam War scarred so many Americans—and scars that deep are passed down to subsequent generations.

Those NVA veterans absolutely had every right to observe and celebrate their day. The fact that it bothered me was the real awakening, cementing my realization that our American identity is forever imprinted upon us.

Huế

Our central visit continued in the vibrant mid-sized city of Huế, featuring quintessential French colonial architecture, charming shops and eateries, and landscaped squares with the requisite socialist-style monuments and sculptures.

With its intricate railings, balconies, shutters, and multiple stories, The Minh Châu building in Huế is a classic example of French Colonial architecture.

Small altars with offerings are set up outside many homes and businesses throughout Vietnam.

Upon exiting the hotel one morning, our group was led to awaiting bicycle rickshaws, one for each of us. I politely declined, opting to walk to our destination. Our guide told me that to refuse would insult my driver, who wanted to earn his fare. I relented, but felt weirdly self-conscious the entire ride, like some mollycoddled royal literally riding on the back of her subject. I climbed aboard, nodding embarrassingly to my grinning, muscled driver. As I was pedaled across the Cầu Trường Tiền Bridge spanning the Perfume River, I hoped the locals in their cars would fail to notice our procession of spoilt Westerners being shamelessly pampered.

Thankfully, the ride was brief, and we soon arrived at the Dông Ba Marketplace. Public food markets are abundant in Vietnam, and

Dried seafood, meat, fruits, and nuts are common Vietnamese snacks and widely available.

can range from a few piles of vegetables along a tiny village roadside to entire neighborhoods of jam-packed vendors within crowded cities. Some are indoor, some are outdoor, but most are a hybrid of the two, and are stocked with everything from baskets of gingerroot to tanks of live squid. As a prolific home cook, I longed for access to a kitchen equipped with all my preferred gastronomic paraphernalia, but had to settle for merely feasting my eyes.

One bewildering trait of the Đông Ba Market in particular was the presence of motorbikes maneuvering among the shoppers, their riders artfully dodging those of us intent on perusing the goods. Also surprising was the myriad of raw meats, fish, and prepared foods left uncovered in the heat. Even with this seemingly unhygienic display, buyers looked healthy and eager to purchase. It was a phenomenon I observed nationwide, leading me to theorize that Vietnamese immune systems have evolved to safeguard against bacteria that would leave Westerners in the fetal position on sweat-soaked sheets, suffering frequent dashes to fluorescently lit hotel commodes.

It is common to see multiple varieties of the same type of produce, such as these shallots and garlic bulbs, offered by the same marketplace vendor.

While driving to our destinations in the Huế area, we were treated to the dramatic scenery of the A Lưới Mountains, an area severely affected by environmental tactics during the War. As a refuge for the Việt Cộng and a vital crossing for the Hồ Chí Minh Trail, the region was subjected to intensive Agent Orange herbicide spraying and bombings, including napalm, by U.S. and South Vietnamese troops. However, the Việt Cộng were not innocent of the area's destruction, using heavy construction equipment to destroy large tracts of jungle for roads and buildings. While nature has

Coconuts are harvested and sold year-round in Vietnam, and shelling, opening, and peeling them is hard work.

A few of our group spoke to this friendly merchant in Huế's Đông Ba Market, where she told us about her 60 years of coming to work, mainly to socialize with her fellow vendors. She said the friendships reward her with a happy, long life.

reclaimed and replenished some swaths of forest, the area still faces severe environmental concerns, including lingering dioxin contamination from Agent Orange and ongoing deforestation for cash crops like coffee and rubber.

Our travelers enjoy one of the many family-style lunches we were served during our tour. In almost every instance, the food was fresh, tasty, and authentic.

The grand staircase leads to the resting place of Emperor Khải Định, the final imperial tomb built for the mighty Nguyễn Dynasty in Huế.

Đức Mẹ La Vang (Our Lady of La Vang Basilica)

At the request of Kevin, a Roman Catholic deacon, we made a group pilgrimage to Our Lady of La Vang. The basilica and surrounding sanctuary grounds sit 40 kilometers (about 25 miles) north of Huế in Quảng Trị Province, where an apparition of the Virgin Mary was reportedly seen in 1798. Vietnam is home to seven million Roman Catholics (7.4% of the population). The religion was introduced by Spanish and Portuguese missionaries in the 16th century and was later evangelized by the French.

Our Lady of La Vang Basilica is an important pilgrimage site for Catholics both in Vietnam and worldwide. It has been rebuilt several times throughout the centuries, and in August 2023, a new basilica was dedicated, just after our visit. Although we were not able to view the inside of the structure, we could clearly view its exterior: an intriguing, square-shaped modern cathedral with a pagoda-style roof, set on a massive plateau. It was strikingly different

Đức Mẹ La Vang, or Our Lady of La Vang Catholic Cathedral, is located in Hải Lăng district, Quảng Trị province, central Vietnam. The name "La Vang" is derived from the phrase meaning "crying out."

from the stone churches and soaring cathedrals built in Vietnam by the colonial French.

We also toured the beautifully landscaped grounds, featuring small chapels, gardens, fountains, and several unique sculptures.

The original church and grounds were destroyed in 1972 during the Vietnam War. Only the historic bell tower remains, a relic that contrasts sharply with the newly rebuilt modernist landscape and structures.

One noteworthy set of statuary featured Mary holding baby Jesus in a stylized tree, representing how they reportedly appeared in the apparition. The faces and postures of Mary, Jesus, and other statues

Created in Italy of Italian marble by Vietnamese sculptor Văn Nhân, the basilica's central statue features a pioneering design by portraying Mary and Jesus in traditional Vietnamese attire. Prior to this depiction, Our Lady of La Vang figures were only shown with European features and clothing. Large structures surrounding the figures are the banyan trees under which the apparition reportedly appeared.

all evoked the style of the Buddhist, Taoist, and Confucianist idols we had seen, with simple, serene, almost comic-book-like features. Yet, rather than being clothed in bright red and surrounded by ornate gold, they sported the compulsory sky blue and white that accompany the Virgin Mary in Western images. Non-human ele-

Another sculpture on the basilica grounds depicts Mary and Jesus in traditional Vietnamese attire. Its style is strikingly reminiscent of Quan Âm, the bodhisattva of compassion, with the child symbolizing her role as a maternal figure.

ments were very contemporary and almost abstract in style, indicative of the sculptures and monuments I had seen in every city and town in Vietnam. In essence, Vietnamese Catholicism displayed its own unique aesthetics that integrated both traditional Vietnamese and Roman Catholic styles.

Fort Evans, Firebase Nancy, and the DMZ

Our tour soon shifted to several war history sites, including two that are now empty fields: Camp Evans, a former U.S. Marine and Army base about 24 kilometers northwest of Huế, and Firebase Nan-

Our group visits the 17th Parallel, the former line that divided North and South Vietnam between 1954 and 1976.

cy, a former U.S. Army and ARVN (Army of the Republic of South Vietnam) fire support base. One would never know these places were once large and active military epicenters, as we found no markers or plaques. It bothered some of our vets to see their recollection of these bustling hubs reduced to forgotten barrenness. One of our vets, Charles, had even been stationed at Firebase Nancy. It was a stark reminder to him—and all of us—that the country has long since moved on from the war forged so solidly—and presently—on their minds.

Next, we headed north to the Hiền Lương Bridge crossing the Bến Hải River. For 21 years during the War, the river divided North and South Vietnam and marked the center of the demilitarized zone (DMZ). Today, the crossing is commemorated with a large brutalist sculpture, a flag tower and mural, and a painted dividing line across

A flag and mural commemorate the former division of the country.

This large sculpture, entitled the "Monument of Desire for National Unification," represents the families separated by the political divide of the War. The spiky towers behind the figures create an imposing scene in the Brutalist architectural style. It was installed in 2018.

the footbridge. It was a surprisingly quiet area, with us being the only people touring this significant historical location.

Cồn Tiên

Located near the DMZ and just two miles from the North Vietnamese border, Cồn Tiên was a vital U.S. Marine base. As home of 1st Battalion, 9th Marines, it joined the bases at Gio Linh, Đông Hà, and Cam Lộ to form the infamous "Leatherneck Square." Some of the heaviest fighting of the War took place in this small but crucial 54-square-mile delineation.

Because many operations were launched from Cồn Tiên, it was subjected to some of the heaviest shelling of the War. Cồn Tiên means "Hill of Angels" in Vietnamese, and the year-long series of brutal battles was often referred to as "Hell on the Hill of Angels."

Cồn Tiên was designated a "Free-Kill Zone" or "Free-Fire Zone" during the War. This designation gave the military the authority to

Ed and Colleen after climbing "The Hill of Angels."

Ed stands at the entrance of one of the few remaining bunkers at Cồn Tiên. Located in Quảng Trị Province, Cồn Tiên was a significant Marine Corps Combat Base and perhaps the most important strongpoint along the DMZ.

fire on anyone or anything without permission for engagement. This strategy was adopted when the perceived risk of enemy presence outweighed the risk of causing collateral damage. As a result, villagers and all other local inhabitants were forced to vacate their homes.

American media coverage from CBS and *Life Magazine* at the site brought combat reality home to American audiences. Approximately 1,419 Marines were killed and 9,265 wounded at Cồn Tiên, with over 7,500 NVA soldiers killed and 168 captured.

Rubber tree farms with colonial origins still remain around Cồn Tiên where French companies, like Michelin, established vast plantations to extract latex. During the War, the plantations became crucial strategic areas, with heavy fighting between U.S. forces and Việt Cộng often occurring amid the rows of trees.

This is likely a rusty American M-113 Armored Personnel Carrier, or a U.S. Marine Corps LVT-2 or LVT-4 (landing vehicle, tracked), which our guide spotted off the road as our group traveled through the DMZ. Many of these vehicles of war were abandoned or destroyed, eventually becoming overgrown with jungle vegetation.

Yet, as with many former battlegrounds we visited, the site of Cồn Tiên shows little evidence of its historical significance. Without our knowledgeable guide and tenacious driver who steered our van several miles along a bumpy dirt road, we would never have found the trail leading to the site.

To get to the bunkers, our guide, my dad, and I climbed a steep rise through the jungle and then walked alongside steers grazing in a rubber tree orchard. There are only a couple of bunkers still standing, unmarked and overgrown with dense thickets of thorny vegetation. We observed a moment of silent contemplation as my dad paid tribute to his fellow Marines who made the final sacrifice in this spot. As I imagined the violent clashes and death that occurred there, it was eerily quiet, save for a soft rustle of leaves and a cow bell in the distance.

Khê Sanh Airfield and Combat Base

The former Khê Sanh Combat Base, just south of the DMZ, offered a better taste of war history, as it had more to offer and was easier for our entire group to access. It was bright and sunny when we drove to the site, but fortunately, not sweltering. As a bonus, we were treated to a scenic view along the drive. The narrow entrance road was surrounded by orchards of lush coffee bean shrubs that waved a greeting in the breeze. I reckoned this welcome contrasted greatly to that of the Marine reinforcements who arrived when these fields were ravaged by the machinery of war.

Located just outside the village of the same name, the base was established by U.S. Army Special Forces in 1962 to monitor the border and prevent North Vietnamese Army (NVA) infiltration into the South.

Although there were several enemy attacks on Khê Sanh and operations launched prior to it, it is best known for its pivotal role during the 1968 Tết Offensive. While initially surprising the U.S. military and allies, the offensive was an overall strategic defeat for the North Vietnamese, as its goal of seizing the base and sparking southern uprisings and defections did not materialize.

A well-preserved Bell UH-1H Iroquois "Huey" helicopter on display at Khê Sanh.

This M48A3 Patton was the primary tank used by the U.S. Army and Marine Corps during the War. The tank features a 90 mm main gun and was the first U.S. medium tank with a four-man crew. To the right of the tank is an M113 armored personnel carrier (APC), used to safely transport troops across combat zones.

Although Khê Sanh was successfully defended and the Tết Offensive was a failure for the North, the operation drew international media attention. It also proved a turning point for the American public, who had previously been led to believe that the North was weak and close to defeat. However, military officials then reported that 200,000 more soldiers and the activation of the reserves were required to win the War.

Some historians also believe that the siege of Khê Sanh distracted the Americans and South Vietnamese enough to allow the Việt Cộng to build up its forces in the South.

The attack began on January 21, prior to the main Tết offensive, when 20,000 enemy troops surrounded 6,000 allied defenders. Although there was never a major ground assault on the base, many small-scale skirmishes occurred along outlying positions. Besieged allies were subjected to heavy mortar, artillery, and rocket bombardment, and American aircraft conducted massive airstrikes in its defense.

A recreated trench and bunker at Khê Sanh.

Ray, Kevin, and Charles pose in front of a Huey.

The Boeing CH-47A or "Chinook" helicopter is a heavy lifter with tandem rotors designed in the late 1950s and used extensively throughout the War to move troops, artillery, ammunition, and supplies. It has a top speed of 170 knots (200 mph) and is powered by two turboshaft engines. This design eliminates the need for anti-torque tail rotors, allowing all power to be used for lift and thrust. This beast can lift up to 26,000 pounds and operate at up to 20,000 feet.

The siege ended on April 8, and the base was dismantled and closed in July 1968 after its strategic position was reevaluated. It was reactivated in 1971 to support the South Vietnamese invasion of Laos but abandoned again that same year. In March 1972, a U.S. Air Force AC-130 gunship was shot down by a PAVN missile over the base, one of only six lost during the War. By March of 1973, PAVN troops had completely seized the base and rebuilt the airstrip.

The siege resulted in 274 U.S. troop deaths and approximately 2,500 wounded, with PAVN casualties and wounded reported as 2,270, though likely higher due to American air and artillery strikes.

The long, fierce battle and resulting victory are an important page in Marine Corps history, and to many, the site is considered sacred ground. Dad told me that if a Marine is introducing him to another Marine says, "Joe is a Khê Sanh Marine," you know you are being introduced to a man who's been to hell and back.

Khê Sanh Airfield and Combat Base is now primarily a large outdoor field with several rebuilt bunkers, trenches, and other fortifications. There are both crumbling and intact buildings, including a chow hall. Several vehicles are on display in different states of preservation. I was first drawn to examine the helicopters: a Bell UH-1 Iroquois "Huey" and a Boeing Ch-47 "Chinook."

I felt like I was on a movie set while walking around the Huey. These choppers were considered the workhorses of the War, performing a variety of roles, including medevac missions (which they were originally designed for during the Korean War), transporting troops into battle, and perhaps most importantly, as attack and defense helicopters. To infantry Marines like my dad, a Huey, the pilot, and M-60 gunner were part of the team that kept them alive.

In contrast, the Chinooks were bigger, stronger, bulkier, and as a result, less maneuverable. They were used for hauling massive loads of cargo, including downed aircraft and mass casualties. The largest Chinook model used in Vietnam had a hefty weight capacity of 46,000 pounds.

I believe I was able to identify at least two other vehicles: an M48 Patton and an M41 or M42 "Duster" anti-aircraft gun (also called a

Ed stands behind a Lockheed C-130A Hercules transport aircraft, just like the one that first brought him to Vietnam as a young Marine.

An original photograph on display at the Khê Sanh Base museum needs no further explanation.

Firedragon). Next to the M48 was an M113 APC (armored personnel carrier), and the two looked like an inseparable, matching set.

By far the most imposing sight was the Lockheed C-130 Hercules cargo and transport plane sitting on the remains of an airstrip. Dad said it was just like the one he arrived in when he first came to 'Nam as an FNG. The plane's versatility and ability to land on uneven, small clearings made it crucial for supporting ground troops and delivering supplies. The C-130 was also adapted into variant models including the AC-130 heavily armed gunship, the MC-130 special operations aircraft able to fly at low altitude, and the KC-130 for aerial refueling missions.

There's a small museum on-site that includes a wartime photo exhibit, maps of attack plans, and glass cases of war paraphernalia, including artillery, small weaponry, tactical gear, and other kit supplies. Like all war history museums and displays we visited, we had to grin and bear the anti-American propaganda (such as cartoons of U.S. Marines depicted as cowering and fearful against the freedom-loving Northern Army).

A Soviet Degtyaryov DP-27 light machine gun on display at the Khê Sanh Base museum. This was the standard-issue Soviet light machine gun used during World War II, with subsequent use among Communist-aligned forces in the Korean and Vietnam Wars.

It was a casual atmosphere, with a couple of nonchalant, non-uniformed caretakers lounging about near the tiny café area, and I got the feeling that most items were for sale and negotiable. I bought a kilo of coffee harvested from the surrounding fields, eager to taste its freshness and support the current use of the surrounding landscape.

If we had the cash, I wondered if we could have bought the C-130 (including a pilot with defection on his mind) to fly us all back home without the hassle of airports. We had to settle for Dad "buying back" his standard-issue Marine canteen.

Before exiting the grounds, I stopped and turned in a slow circle for a 360-degree view of the valley and overlooking hills. I pictured myself as a young Marine, knowing we were heavily outnumbered and surrounded by thousands of NVA eyes looking down on us. I saw reinforcement troops arriving by chopper, dodging artillery and encumbered with gear packs as they ran for cover. My mind's eye transformed this tranquil and lush land into a ravaged hellscape, with my ears ringing and my world on fire.

Walking back to the bus with Ray, we met an old local holding mud-caked medals and campaign pins in an outstretched palm. His back was bent and his clothes tattered, his hands rough and dirty from digging. We each bought an NVA medal. Our grateful seller gave us both a bow, a wink, and a broad smile that showed off a sparkling gold tooth.

Monkey Mountain and Marble Mountain Facilities

While in Đà Nẵng and its environs, our guide pointed out two sites that were significant to Dad's very first assignment as a Marine in-country. Sơn Trà Mountain, or "Monkey Mountain," is a mountain and peninsula range overlooking the Bay of Đà Nẵng and the East Sea. During the War, the mountain housed a U.S. military communications facility in close proximity to the Marble Mountain Air Facility, where many aircraft crashes occurred. When Dad's platoon first arrived, it was assigned to patrol the mountain to keep the VC from getting close enough to use mortars and small arms fire to attack the base.

Part of the Marble Mountain range, a cluster of five protruding mountains named after the five elements of Taoism: metal, wood, fire, water, and earth.

In 1977, the site was deemed a natural reserve with protected forests for endangered species, but sadly, it has more recently seen a wave of significant, illegal development spurred by corrupt local officials.

Linh Ứng Pagoda Complex

It's somewhat ironic but quintessentially Vietnamese that Monkey Mountain, with its violent history and current environmental challenges, is now home to perhaps the most hallowed Buddhist sanctuary in the country. Construction of the Linh Ứng Pagoda Complex began in 2004 and was dedicated six years later, in 2010. It is highlighted by a 67-meter (220-foot) Quan Âm statue and offers panoramic views of Đà Nẵng, the East Sea, and the surrounding mountains.

Although as tall as a 30-story building, I did not find the Quan Âm statue imposing. While I had to crane my neck to look upon her serene face, she seemed to project a calming influence upon the vast area she overlooked. I believe this goddess of mercy is not to be regarded in awe and fear, but in love and reverence.

The Linh Ứng Pagoda complex on the Sơn Trà Peninsula offers stunning panoramic views, landscaped gardens, ornate pagodas, and a towering Lady Buddha, making it a premier Buddhist destination in Vietnam.

The famous Quan Âm statue stands 67 meters (220 feet) high atop a 35-meter lotus platform and is the tallest in Vietnam. The statue was reportedly constructed from a single piece of white marble sourced from the nearby Non Nước Marble Village.

The pagoda, each layer symbolizing another step closer to divine enlightenment, sits at the other end of the complex. Like the other structures on-site, it embraces a harmonious combination of traditional and contemporary architecture. While its design can be seen throughout Vietnam, its unusual coloring pays tribute to nature, with green roofs echoing the mountains, and blue and white accents, the sky and sea. I could tell that much consideration went

A visitor could spend hours strolling the complex's gorgeous grounds, which are open daily and offer free admission.

Wild pigs seem to be rather tame in Vietnam, as no one appeared concerned about this varmint strolling through the courtyard.

into the placement of all outdoor elements in the complex, with luminous white statues, including Quan Âm, framed by the sparkling sea or lush mountains from all angles. Large potted bonsai displays were interspersed among the statuary, edged by a canopy of larger trees, boulders, and fountains that seemed to meld into the surrounding rock formations and distant highlands. Softly colored, tiled walkways beckoned visitors to the next display. My parents even saw a wild boar casually trotting by (of which no one seemed to bat an eyelash, underscoring the harmonious vibe).

I'm eternally thankful that the complex was on our itinerary, and I appreciate why some consider it a Buddhist paradise on Earth.

Đồi A Bia (Hamburger Hill)

For me, a highlight of our central tour was climbing Hamburger Hill, officially called Đồi A Bia, where a bloody 10-day battle occurred in May 1969 resulting in 72 U.S. soldiers killed and 372 wounded. The battle resulted in an estimated 630 North Vietnamese deaths. Journalists interviewed a U.S. sergeant who compared the casualties to the inside of a hamburger machine, and the gruesome moniker stuck. The battle was also portrayed in a popular

Ed and our guide, Anh-Co, sitting on some of the more intact steps of Hamburger Hill, or Đồi A Bia.

One of the historical directional signs along our ascent of Hamburger Hill.

1987 film entitled *Hamburger Hill*, often cited as one of the most realistic movies about the Vietnam War.

Đồi A Bia (meaning Crouching Beast Mountain) is a lone peak located in the A Shầu Valley, only a mile from the Laotian border. It is the site of a controversial campaign during the War, as part of a sweep of the valley to cut off North Vietnamese infiltration from Laos and secure protection for the cities of Huế and Đà Nẵng. It took 11 attacks for the American and South Vietnamese forces to secure the hill. But just five days after the hard-won victory, it was abandoned because of its lack of strategic value. The North Vietnamese reoccupied the hill a month later.

U.S. General Melvin Zais, who led the assault, was quoted as saying "The only significance of the hill was that your North Vietnamese were on it . . . the hill itself had no tactical significance." Media coverage of the battle contributed to an outpouring of anti-war sentiment in the U.S., and Senator Edward Kennedy condemned the battle as "senseless and irresponsible."

Although General Zais disagreed that the battle was a wasted effort, calling it a "tremendous, gallant victory," the Nixon Administration subsequently ordered the commanding generals to avoid these types of intense ground battles.

An offering of incense and flowers adorn a memorial plaque, written in Vietnamese, at the top of Hamburger Hill.

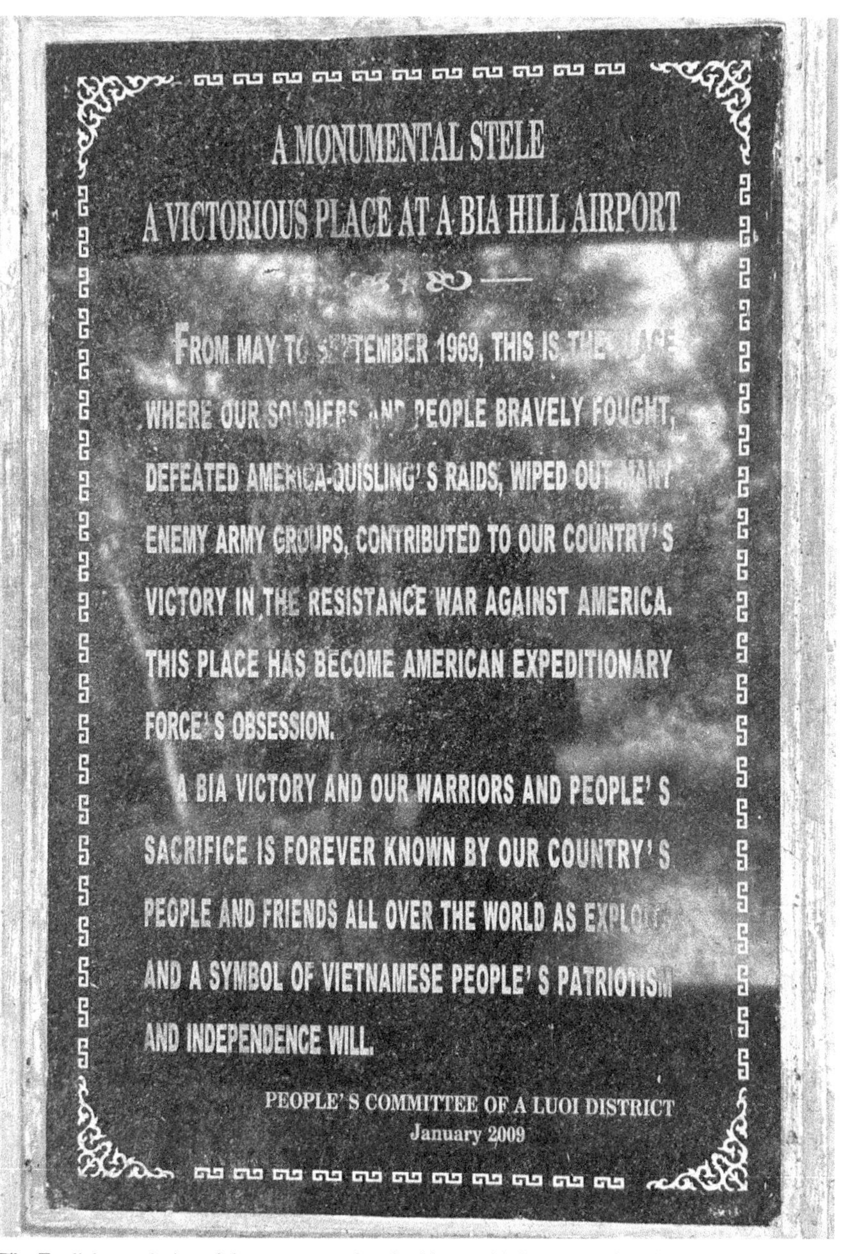

The English translation of the monument, laced with one-sided propaganda (although the "obsession" accusation proved to be accurate).

Scaling the hill was a physical challenge, certainly warranting a victory fist pump.

I did not realize it at the time, but climbing Hamburger Hill played a vital role in my visit to Vietnam. The hike is over four miles to the summit, which sits at 3,074 feet (937 meters), and visitors are required to obtain a guide and permit. The terrain, as expected, was steep and uneven, so only our guide Anh-Cơ, Dad, and I climbed the hill. The incline was a wide trail surrounded by dense jungle, with some areas offering a steady stream of broken rock "steps." It was a hot and exhausting climb, and we stopped a few times along the way to take a breather. The fact that I was fighting a respiratory infection did not help matters, but there was no tomorrow. I climbed Hamburger Hill that day, or not at all.

At one point I lagged behind my dad and our guide. I was alone in the jungle, imagining myself as a wide-eyed American draftee surrounded by these unfamiliar sensations. Even with my stuffy nose, I could recognize the scent of unfamiliar vegetation. My eyes adjusted to the long, sharp sunbeams piercing the shadowed canopy above. But most alien of all was the overwhelming cacophony of cicadas. I had heard swarms before in our temperate forests at home,

Charles and Agnes pose at the base of Hamburger Hill.

but this was something else entirely. As I remained still, my threat to them eliminated, the insects became so deafening that even a close conversation would have been impossible. I wondered how a greenie from a place like Tucson or Los Angeles kept his sanity intact while trying to get some shuteye in the bush or a foxhole.

Not surprisingly, there was sparse evidence of Đồi A Bia's historical significance, other than a couple of old signs pointing out the location of a former helicopter crash site and an enemy (American) fortification. But the top of the hill did feature a well-kept pagoda erected in 2009, with a stone plaque engraved in Vietnamese on one side and English on the other. The message speaks of the site being home to a "victorious place where our soldiers and people bravely fought, defeated America-Quisling's Raids…" ("Quisling" in this case refers to those who collaborated with the Americans, such as the South Vietnamese Army). The plaque's biased inscription was apparent to any Western visitor familiar with our military history of the controversial battle, and I could tell by his face that it troubled my dad a bit to read the words.

Although our climb up Hamburger Hill ended with another reminder of what many consider an American military debacle, I was satisfied that I was able to make this monumental trek with my dad. It was a hard climb for both of us, and I believe that reaching the summit was our small tribute to those who suffered intensely violent deaths while fighting for the ownership of this hill. It was a case of misguided zeal on the part of military brass, but as is often the reality, it was the infantry grunts who suffered the consequences.

Vịnh Mốc Tunnel System

The Vịnh Mốc tunnel complex is an impressive hand-dug system that hugs the coastline of the South China Sea. During the War, the villages of Sơn Trung and Sơn Hạ were regularly bombed by the American military due to their location just north of the DMZ. In 1966, the villagers began digging the tunnels to escape the destruction, and sources report anywhere from 60-90 families living underground for the duration of the War. The limestone tunnels include a ventilation system, large rooms that housed entire

Ed exits one of the tunnels at Vịnh Mốc. Unlike the Củ Chi tunnels, which were primarily used for combat operations, the Vịnh Mốc tunnels were used to shelter the local population from U.S. aerial bombardment.

Mannequins depict the confined areas inhabited by families in the tunnels.

Traversing the tunnels.

families, dining areas with wells, latrines, and even a hospital. The three levels of tunnels, running for almost two kilometers with a depth up to 30 meters, are bleak, dim, and slippery. It is said that 17 babies were born in the tunnels.

An original photograph on display in the tunnel museum illustrates how babies were housed in makeshift nurseries.

One of the tunnel exits led us to a beautiful shoreline, underscoring what the villagers had to give up to survive.

Today, the complex includes a small museum with a map of the tunnel system and photos and relics of daily life underground. The only modern updates inside the tunnels themselves are the dim electric bulbs and posed mannequins displaying the incredible ingenuity and endurance of the Vietnamese civilian. One tunnel we traversed led to an exit with an expansive view of the turquoise South China Sea, further underscoring the contrasting underground existence the villagers were forced to choose in order to survive.

Hôi An

One of the most anthropologically significant regions we visited in Vietnam was the Ancient Quarter of the city of Hôi An, a UNESCO World Heritage site. A busy and prosperous coastal port town that thrived from the 16th to 19th centuries, Hôi An features cultural and architectural influences from the countries that traded there—primarily China, Japan, and France. We strolled through charming neighborhoods in a melting pot of styles, including Chinese wood-

The entrance to the Quan Âm Pagoda in Hội An's Ancient Town follows the design and color of the surrounding architecture.

The front gates of the Chinese Fujian Assembly Hall are a significant example of the fusion between Chinese and Vietnamese styles in Hội An. The hall was built in 1690 as a gathering place for Chinese merchants, and later became a temple dedicated to the deity Thiên Hậu, the goddess of the sea who protects sailors.

Our group relaxes at the Museum of Traditional Medicine in Hội An.

Everywhere we ate, the servers and staff were friendly, helpful, and attentive.

A scenic view of Lăng Cô Bay with the Trường Sơn Mountains in the background, a popular stop between Huế and Đà Nẵng. The blue structures are platforms supporting the local oyster farming industry.

Traditional fishing boats docked along Đầm Lập An, a lagoon situated near the Hải Vân Pass, known for its misty mountains and panoramic coastlines.

The weather was perfect for our leisurely ride along the Hoài River.

Captain Ray took a turn at the wheel.

en shops, Japanese pagodas and bridges, vibrant French colonial homes, and the quintessential Vietnamese "tube" houses, akin to multi-floored and extremely narrow row homes. We peeked into small shops bursting with colorful goods, busy cafés, and fashionable art galleries on streets interspersed with canals, all spanned by

A traditional fishing vessel.

Basket boat tours at the edge of the Bảy Mẫu Coconut Forest in Hội An offer tourists a fun and rowdy adventure. Our group delighted in the raucous laughter and festive music coming from the scene.

red-arched Japanese footbridges. We passed marketplaces heaped with prepared local foods and produce.

After exploring the town, we savored a fabulous lunch at a garden restaurant along the Hoài River, then boarded a wooden

Our group was fortunate to meet a family who cooked a traditional lunch for us in their own home near Hội An.

Mary and Karen share a drink with the family patriarch. "Một, hai, ba, vô," is a common toast meaning "one, two, three, in!"

riverboat painted vivid red and turquoise. We slowly motored along, enjoying views of the surrounding hills and fishing trawler crews gathering nets of fish. We passed by a festive group of Chinese tourists enjoying riverside cocktails and loud pop music, and we laughed *with* them as they precariously boarded and attempted to navigate several ubiquitous "coconut boats." We continued along in our own more seaworthy vessel, eventually disembarking at a small village which acted as a haven for local soldiers during the War, and now exports seafood products to the surrounding area.

Our host showed us how soybeans are easily ground into soft tofu, which he served with honey for dessert.

Our hotel in Hôi An echoed the pictorial beauty of the surrounding area, with a decadent garden pool and grounds rife with tropical foliage. During this leg of the journey, we also got to meet a local family who cooked and served us dinner in their home. We

A snippet of Đà Nẵng's Nguyễn Văn Trỗi pedestrian bridge in the foreground, with a partial view of the famous Dragon Bridge behind it. Both span the Han River, while the Dragon Bridge connects the city center to its coastal areas. On Saturday and Sunday nights at 9 p.m., the dragon's head shoots jets of fire and water.

Mỹ Khê Beach was known as "China Beach" to American and Australian soldiers during the War. The 20-mile stretch of fine white sand and turquoise surf is located on Đà Nẵng's eastern shore. Ed visited during the War, approaching via a small dirt road—a stark contrast to the well-traveled highway that gave our group access.

sampled local delicacies made by a mother and her two daughters in their kitchen, and then watched the father grind fresh soybeans into tofu and serve it to us drizzled with honey from his own hives for a refreshing dessert. It was a truly unique and hospitable experience to visit this kind and welcoming family. I even got a lesson in grinding my own soybeans!

The South

Sài Gòn (Hồ Chí Minh City)

The final leg of our journey began with a short flight from Đà Nẵng to Hồ Chí Minh City, still referred to as Sài Gòn by many. As soon as our van left the airport, it was easy to surmise that Sài Gòn was a much larger and more modern city than the historic and subdued Hà Nội. The number of speeding, weaving motorbikes defied logic. Graffiti-defaced slums were adjacent to streets of international department stores. Eateries of every size and cuisine

Sài Gòn, officially called Hồ Chí Minh City, is Vietnam's largest city with a municipality population of over 14 million in 2025.

beckoned with flashing neon. Just like everywhere in Vietnam—city, suburb, or village—tidy public squares centered around modernist sculptures.

Hồ Chí Minh City had an imposing urban core of spouting fountains, plaques, and sculptures hailing communist heroes. Flags and banners flew over orderly green spaces and massive government buildings. Not a speck of trash could be found in this section. Yet everywhere else in town, virtually everything was for sale—as if to say, "This is still the capitalist part of the country." Like its two names, the city seemed to have two opposing personalities.

After settling into our gleaming, modern accommodations, we were free to explore this very walkable city. I headed out on my own, happy to have some solo time and to stretch my legs after a day of travel. The street adjacent to our hotel beckoned me. It was a taste of Europe in the middle of this dense Asian city, with its Easter-egg basket of sprawling French colonial mansions tucked behind a towering line of ancient plane trees.

This peaceful stroll abruptly led me to a sprawling outdoor marketplace. Typical of city life, the juxtaposition between wealth and

Everyone rides motorbikes.

The "Monument to the Workers' Struggle" is a Socialist Realist–style sculpture located on a roundabout in Sài Gòn.

poverty, and chaos and serenity, was commonplace in Sài Gòn. But one rarity was that I felt safe wherever I went. Unlike in the U.S., violent crime is extremely rare in Vietnam, and crimes committed with guns are nonexistent. I think it's also important to point out that I felt a safer *vibe*. Although as a traveler I am always a bit on my guard, I never felt like prey as I have in sketchy neighborhoods back home. Maybe it was the lack of leering or unwelcome glares that lone women strollers often encounter. People let me be, but were respectful when approached. I also never saw one cop when walking around. People were relaxed and behaved themselves, yet they did not seem fearful. Dare I say they seemed . . . present, or even *mind-*

ful, as their theology teaches? Whatever the underlying reason, I was able to decompress and fully enjoy the scenery more than I ever have when walking alone in a new city.

The next morning, I woke up with the sun and decided to head out before breakfast. Walking along the famous Đồng Khởi Street

Sài Gòn is filled with charming alleyways housing small cafes, pubs, and boutiques.

Plane trees line a street of French Colonial-style homes in Sài Gòn.

transported me, once again, back to the days of French colonialism. As if to reinforce its status as an undeniable world capital, Sài Gòn's grand avenue is reminiscent of European cities, lined with a number of well-known colonial landmarks, including several palatial hotels, trendy cafes, and luxury shops. My first stop was The Hôtel Continental, a gathering place for foreign journalists during both the

For a small additional fee, many vendors will clean your fish, meat, or produce.

Produce vendors are never deterred by a little rain.

First and Second Indochina Wars. Journalist and author Hunter S. Thompson, one of my all-time favorites, stayed there while documenting the Fall of Sài Gòn for *Rolling Stone* Magazine in 1975. I also caught a glimpse of The Grand Hotel, setting for much of Graham Greene's Vietnam-War-era novel *The Quiet American.* This strenuous solo stroll cleared my head and helped me mentally prepare for the day ahead, filled with war history and much togetherness.

Củ Chi Tunnels

Our guide for this southern leg was the young Thành, a baby-faced local with a quick smile, quiet wit, and a plethora of optimism. He and our driver collected us after breakfast for the short van ride to the famed Củ Chi Tunnels Memorial Park, just northwest of Sài Gòn. The tunnels, first built by communist rebels in the 1940s during the First Indochina War against the French colonialists, are part of a vast underground network that runs throughout much of the country.

During much of the Vietnam War, including the 1968 Tết Offensive, the Cù Chi tunnels were expanded by the Việt Cộng and became their base of operations. As the Americans heavily relied on aerial bombing during the War, the tunnels became a refuge for village life as well as a planning center for communist combat operations against nearby Sài Gòn. Việt Cộng and NVA troops also launched effective "Strike and Disappear" strategies from the tunnels, where they attacked and then retreated back underground when faced with heavy counterattacks. The tunnels and area forests were part of the area known as the Iron Triangle, where frequent operations rendered Sài Gòn's outskirts highly insecure to American troops and allies.

Many tunnels ran beneath the Michelin Rubber Plantations, and it was widely believed among soldiers that U.S. forces were under an informal agreement with the French-owned company to avoid heavy air and artillery strikes that might destroy the valuable rubber trees. While records indicate that support was occasionally

Our guide, Thành, explains a partial model of the tunnels.

A worker demonstrates how the Việt Cộng hid the tunnel entrances.

used, the perception of these restrictions contributed to the tactical challenges posed by the Củ Chi Tunnels.

Numerous booby traps were set above the tunnels to capture, maim, or kill American and ARVN troops. Dad explained to us how his platoon often came across VC fighters who would pop up out of the tunnels, fire an AK-47, and disappear back into the

An exhibit of American bombs and shells at the Củ Chi Tunnels historic site.

ground, completely undetected. Even if no one was hit, this action forced Marines to suspend or delay operations to search for the enemy. This chaotic tactic was partnered with the gruesome consequences of trap setting that haunted American ground troops. Made of bamboo and undetectable by mine sweeps, these included the infamous "punji trap"–sharpened sticks secured in camouflaged pits and often smeared with urine, feces, or toxic plants to cause infection. The spikes were specifically designed to maim the lower limbs, forcing units to stall while treating or freeing trapped comrades. Many grisly punji trap designs were employed, and we saw displays of the "clipping armpit trap," "rolling spikes," the "fish trap," and the "window trap."

Other common traps included the "mace," a large, spiked metal or wooden ball that would swing down from a tree when triggered; the "tiger trap," similar to the mace, but with a swinging spiked board; the "pressure release trap," often set on war trophies such as Việt Cộng flags that American soldiers liked to collect, or set on wounded or dead American soldiers that corpsmen or medics would try to rescue or recover; and "bamboo whips," long poles pulled into arcs that shot back into a straight position to impale anyone who tripped the wire.

Tires discarded by American and allied forces were collected and made into shoes by the Việt Cộng. Nicknamed Hồ Chí Minh sandals, they were durable, silent, and perfect for the jungle.

Grenades and ammunition were also employed in traps, including grenade safety pins attached to tripwires, grenades in cans with pins pulled and levers released when cans were disturbed, and bullets placed in bamboo tubes with a protruding nail that caused the bullets to detonate when stepped on (called "toe poppers").

Fran and Thành smile for the camera.

This Soviet-made T-54 or T-55 tank on display at the Củ Chi Tunnels historic site was used by the North Vietnamese Army or the Việt Cộng. The hammer and sickle flag represents the alliance between industrial and agricultural workers and their unity in the struggle for a socialist society.

All of these demonstrations and displays were a stark lesson about what Dad's platoon and other American troops encountered in the jungle.

The cunningly devious nature of these traps disturbed me and forced me to examine the nature of the enemy. Việt Cộng guerrilla fighters considered American troops to be invaders of their homeland. I admitted to myself that if my town, my neighborhood, and my family were in danger from a foreign enemy, I too would employ any means necessary to protect them.

Ray, Kevin, and Lou walk around what is likely a towed M114 155mm howitzer field gun and a Lockheed C-130A Hercules transport plane.

An original photo of a female artillery squad at the Củ Chi Tunnels site. Women constituted a large portion of Việt Cộng fighters and served in critical combat and support roles.

The Việt Cộng were masters of setting booby traps, and many original variations are on display at the Củ Chi Tunnels site.

War Remnants Museum, Sài Gòn

Situated in downtown Sài Gòn, the War Remnants Museum is a massive complex that includes a three-story exhibition center and surrounding walled grounds with American War-era planes, helicopters, tanks, and even unexploded ordnance and an F-111 fighter bomber jet.

An M48 Patton tank and a Boeing CH-47 Chinook helicopter are part of the large outdoor display at the War Remnants Museum in Saigon.

A notable courtyard exhibit at the museum is this U.S. Air Force Northrop F-5A fighter jet.

The inside includes both permanent and temporary exhibits, with themed rooms containing countless photographs, documents, maps, video clips, weaponry, munitions, uniforms—a massive catalogue of the legacy of war on the Vietnamese nation.

Ed and Charles examine a wall map inside the museum.

This original photo by Robert Capa, taken moments before he was killed by a landmine during the First Indochina War, highlights the danger faced by war correspondents.

A couple of the museum's former monikers—Museum of Chinese and American War Crimes—and Exhibition House for U.S. and Puppet Crimes—offer a glimpse into its political slant. The institution was not given its current name until 1995 when the Clinton Administration lifted sanctions on Vietnam. According to its website, the museum receives almost a million visitors per year from all over the world. Its stated purpose is to recognize and memorialize the people of Vietnam who have suffered as a consequence of the French Colonial era and the First and Second Indochina Wars, and I believe it achieves that goal, albeit in a biased manner.

Many of its displays are disturbing and emotionally charged, including a section detailing the human effects of Agent Orange, napalm, and white phosphorus employed by the American military. This includes photographs of disfigured children and three jars of preserved human fetuses deformed by dioxins. The Mỹ Lai Massacre (where U.S. soldiers raped, tortured, and massacred a village of unarmed civilians—mostly women, children, and elderly men) is prominently represented. Yet, the exhibit also includes the efforts of the American veteran and the journalist who broke the news, as well as the subsequent American public outcry condemning the massacre. And while most displays feature a North Vietnamese perspective, many of the disturbing photographs of atrocities were provided by U.S. media sources.

One section is dedicated to the imprisonment and torture of political prisoners, and displays "tiger cages," where the South Vietnamese kept political prisoners, and a French guillotine used by colonial forces.

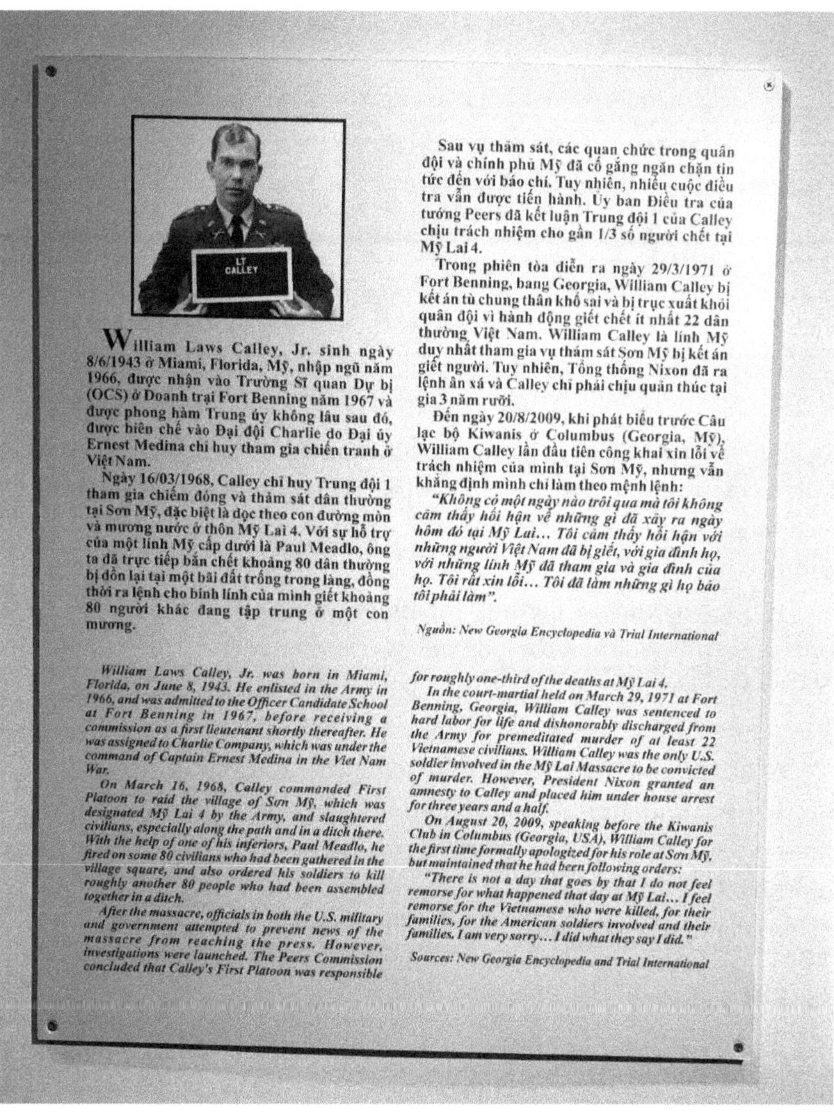

William Lewis Calley, Jr., was the only U.S. soldier to be convicted for the civilian massacre at Mỹ Lai.

In addition to the extensive display regarding the Mỹ Lai massacre, the museum notes the involvement of Lawrence Manley Colburn, who helped end the killings and later testified to what he had witnessed.

An exhibit solely dedicated to journalists on both sides who were killed covering the Second Indochina War was a needed reminder to honor those who die in the service of documenting and reporting history.

While technically factual, the museum can be considered a one-sided propaganda tool for the government of Vietnam, as no North Vietnamese atrocities inflicted on American or South Vietnamese forces or civilians are acknowledged.

Near the exit, there are multiple representations of peace, reconciliation, and anti-war posters from international artists. Yet this museum's documentation of the bitter cost of war is not for the faint of heart. Our group was silent and despondent as we left the property, absorbing the enormity of all we had seen.

Mekong Delta

As we moved south from the epicenter and suburbs of Sài Gòn into the flat terrain of the Mekong Delta, lush rice paddies quickly enveloped us. Known as the Rice Bowl of Vietnam, the Delta

Floating village communities, like this one on the Tiền River in the Mekong Delta, have adapted to life on the water by constructing homes and other structures on floating platforms.

Most boats used in the Delta are made of wood and are commonly painted with vibrant colors.

Large-scale coconut farming is a major industry along the Delta, with a reported 2 million tons produced annually.

produces 90% of the country's rice exports and more than half of its staple food crops. I leaned against the window as we traveled, mesmerized by the endless expanses of bright green. A blade of rice is elegant and soft, and each sways in concert to create a landscape of natural movement with even the gentlest of breezes. After the bustling urbanization of the last couple of days, this sensory shift gave me a serene, even enchanted sensation.

We arrived in the small city of Bến Tre after an approximately two-hour drive, and made our way to the Hùng Vương Pier to meet our boat. Our tour took us along the Bến Tre River, a tributary of the Mekong River. Like most of the boats we saw, it was wooden and brightly painted in multiple colors. It was large enough to warrant a sunshade, had benches along the port and starboard, and a central table that held sliced local fruits and chilled coconuts for our refreshment.

Although we saw one or two other tour boats at the dock, most of the boats on the river were fishing vessels and small barges transporting coconut products, another important industry along the Delta. Our guide explained that all parts of the coconut are used: the water and the meat for food, drink, and body products; and the shell and husk, which are shredded for fuel and woven to

Many homes along the Delta are very modest, yet inhabitants are welcoming and friendly.

make durable coir mats, building and erosion control materials, and handicrafts.

It was still morning as we slowly cruised the river, and brightly colored, handmade fish netting sparkled in the sun. Stark cobalt and turquoise boats echoed the sky, as fiery ruby and saffron nets provided contrast. We observed nets being checked and emptied, then stilted and lowered back into the water. Angler silhouettes completed the scene.

After we docked at a riverside hamlet, repurposed golf carts took us past residential huts to a coconut processing workshop. Here,

Mary enjoys a shot of coconut moonshine, much to the chagrin of Thanh.

The traditional craft of broom making utilizes coconut palm fronds and local grasses and is an important source of income for many rural households in the Delta region.

we sampled and purchased handmade candies and other local coconut products. We visited other village spots that caught our eye, including an all-female broom-making facility, a mat-maker, and a water coconut grower. One striking image I'll always recall was the

A server brings us deep-fried elephant ear fish, a regional delicacy and signature dish of the Delta. The tender white meat is flaked off and wrapped in rice paper with cucumbers and fresh pineapple, then dipped in a variety of sauces.

colorful marble used for raised sarcophagi throughout the village, mined locally. The homes of the living were small and simple, while the dead rested eternally in polished marble, underscoring the importance of ancestor veneration and respect. I feel fortunate to have met these friendly and industrious villagers, sustained by the dense jungle and thriving river surrounding them.

After our ride away from the hamlet, we docked and boarded small sampan boats piloted by smiling locals. It was time for our tour along the Bến Tre River and surrounding canals, and I was excited to experience this famed voyage. Bến Tre is a tributary of the greater Mekong River, and sampan boats are the traditional, and still most common, mode of transport. These flat-bottomed, wooden vessels are easily maneuvered through the river's narrow and shallow waterways.

Mary and her boat captain enjoy the ride and perfect weather.

Our sampan tour along the Delta canals was definitely a trip highlight.

Each of our boats held three passengers and one pilot, whose only tools were an oar and a long stick to help push through the shallows. Our drivers did not speak English, so our ride was silent and serene, with only the dips of the oar and the fluttering of surrounding vegetation making sound. Low-hanging, bright green palm trees enveloped us as we weaved through the canals. The waning sun took on an orange glow as it set, softly backlighting the leaves and grasses. It was a well-planned and calming conclusion to our active day in the Delta.

Before driving back to Sài Gòn, we stopped for dinner at a riverside garden of heavily laden bananas and other ripe fruits, bright blue pea-flower blossoms, and ponds of sacred lotus flowers. I savored every one of the local delicacies in this tropical Eden, including the famous fried "elephant ear" gourami fish served with pineapple, a Tiền Giang lager, and savory shrimp "donuts."

The Mekong Delta and River basin house the world's largest inland fishery and boast the second-highest fish species diversity after the Amazon. It is also home to some of the world's largest fish, including the giant freshwater stingray and Mekong catfish. Sadly, the Delta faces challenges from climate change, overpopulation, pollution, and groundwater extraction. Without proper protections, Vietnam's food security, economy, and the livelihoods of millions of people (like the villagers we met) along with critically endangered native species (like the freshwater Irrawaddy dolphin and Siamese crocodile) are at grave risk. I can only hope that good sense and sustainability overcome greed and corruption, and that this region will still thrive when I return someday. Nevertheless, I was grateful for the opportunity to visit and enjoy this prosperous region, and to allow Mother Earth to renew my brain and lungs with fresh air and mental clarity.

Goodbye Sài Gòn

As usual on my final day of any big trip, I get anxious about seeing as much as I can before departing, knowing I may never pass this way again. I toured with the group, but also set out on my own during any downtime, even if it was just a short jaunt to a quaint alleyway of shops while waiting for lunch to be served. I bought souvenirs and local foodstuffs, took loads of photos, and talked to as many people as I could, soaking in the last of this enchanting country that had wholeheartedly welcomed our motley group of Americans.

Conveniently next to the city's iconic Notre Dame Cathedral (unfortunately under construction during our visit), the Central Post

Sài Gòn is a bustling financial center with a rich history and culture, known for blending historical charm with ultra-modern skyscrapers.

Charles stands in front of the Sài Gòn Central Post Office, whose design is attributed to the famous French architect Marie-Alfred Foulhoux. Charles is an avid philatelist, and was excited to pop in for some additions to his collection.

Although a popular tourist destination and historic landmark, the building is still a fully functioning post office.

Office was a last-day highlight. Built between 1886 and 1901, it's one of the city's oldest buildings, designed by renowned French architect Marie-Alfred Foulhoux. The building features a unique vaulted ceiling and a neo-baroque façade with window frames bearing names of leading scientists and philosophers. The décor is considered a perfect blend of European and Asian ornamentation, but the palmette lanterns and Roman arches first caught my attention as I walked in. My gaze then settled on the large portrait of Uncle Hồ on the back wall, always watching. As this is a working post office, I was able to buy some stamps for my last round of postcards home.

Our next stop was the bustling Bến Thành Marketplace, with its French colonial influence and Art Deco/Neo-Classical structure and clock tower, built between 1912 and 1914. This massive confluence of stalls sells everything from necessary staples to luxury items, including garments, cooked food, handicrafts and art, cheap souvenirs, liquors, raw and packaged herbs and spices, fabrics, coffee and tea, cookware, plants and flowers, and the list goes on. It was a shopper's paradise, and a bit overwhelming. As I walked along the narrow aisles, merchants called out to me, showing their products and offering deals. As I tend to avoid hard sales and can only haggle when in the mood, my purchases were limited. However, at the urging of our guide, I did taste and subsequently purchase the famous Vietnamese weasel coffee, which holds an interesting history.

As native Vietnamese plantation workers were not allowed to drink the coffee owned by their French overlords, they collected beans that were swiped, swallowed, and excreted by wild weasels. After washing (!), roasting, and brewing the beans, they realized that the enzymes in the critter's digestive systems removed all bitterness and created an amazingly smooth and subtle brew. Despite their backdoor route, the beans have become a high-priced delicacy, and are now farmed by weasel workers whose excreted commodity is exported worldwide. Like sausages and hot dogs,

This stand in Sài Gòn's famous Bến Thành Market offers a plethora of shellfish, including black tiger shrimp, giant freshwater prawns, mangrove periwinkle snails, common periwinkle snails, leaping conches, sun clams, and hard clams.

During the day, the Bến Thành Market is a hectic shopping place, but at night, the surrounding area transforms into a social hub featuring shopping, food, drink, and general merriment.

this coffee can only be enjoyed without deep thought of its dubious route to your mouth.

Our very last stop before heading to the airport for our long-haul journey home was a place I requested to see: the Tân Định Parish Catholic Church, or Sacred Heart of Jesus, commonly known as the "Pink Church." First built between 1870 and 1876, it is painted a vivid pink both inside and out, with a blend of Roman, Gothic, and Renaissance architecture. Unfortunately, the barrage of daily tourists has forced officials to close the interior to anyone but regular parishioners, yet the exterior alone was quite a treat, and I appreciated the decision to paint the church the symbolic Catholic color of joy.

As we all carefully packed our fragile purchases and prepared for our seemingly eternal, mind-numbing journey home, I said my final goodbyes to Vietnam. As our jet gathered speed and lifted off the ground, I sincerely hoped I would be back, with my husband

In Vietnam, one eats wherever one can find a small seat.

The stunning Tân Định Church, built in the late 1800s, is one of the oldest and largest Catholic churches in Sài Gòn, alongside the Notre Dame Cathedral.

Our group waves goodbye to Sài Gòn, and Vietnam. It was an epic journey.

and daughter in tow. The need to further explore, revisit favored spots, discover new ones, savor the food, and dwell among the mindful inhabitants was a strong urge. And still is.

Thank you, Vietnam, for your incredible hospitality.

Part Three

The Debrief

An early-morning scene illustrates the dense urban environment of Hà Nội's Old Quarter.

If you continue to carry bricks from your past, you will end up building the same house.

—Stewart Stafford

Veteran Travelers' Reflections on Our Trip

Charles

The trip was not what Charles expected. He thought he'd see more war remnants, but they were all gone. He said he should have thought more about it, should have anticipated this after visiting other former war sites, such as the Fort Sill Apache Prisoner of War Cemetery in New Mexico where Geronimo was held. This was slightly disappointing to him. Although, he added, we did not make it to the town of Vũng Tàu where he was stationed at the R&R center.

Ultimately, it felt like an enjoyable vacation to Charles and his wife Agnes, especially the nice hotels. Although dealing with the intense heat was difficult.

Charles was surprised by several aspects of today's Vietnam, including the masses of motor scooters, the abundance of tour buses, and the fact that a person can buy almost any car make and model. He also did not expect such a wide variety of international foods; you just had to look around. Charles smiled while recalling the little tables and chairs they still have, how they stoop and squat to sit down. That part is the same as when he was there during the War.

He did not expect so many people to speak English, even in the villages. Charles theorized that it's due to all the tourism. The garbage on the streets was the same as it was then, and a sad sight. Maybe it's a little better, he reflected, especially in the cities.

As Americans, Charles was moved by how friendly and helpful the Vietnamese people were to us. Because of the War, he expected them to be bitter. But this was not the case at all.

It was amazing that there was no violence, and no violent crime during our visit. We did not hear about it and did not see it, Charles stressed.

Charles is glad to have seen the country in a time of peace. Even during the War, it was a pretty country, he recalled. He saw some temples and churches back then and was surprised that they were so religious.

Unfortunately, Charles did not gain any type of closure by visiting. My memories are not going to change, he said. Because you keep your memories from way back, and you'll always have them, he explained.

Charles reflected positively on how the country now manages its businesses as a free market. At least that's what it seems to be, he added. It was not so free when he was there in the War. It was much more corrupt, he recalled. Something about what's happening now, it's a dream, mused Charles, how the government lets people be how they are.

Lou

When asked what he expected, Lou said he didn't know, as he's a "wait and see" kind of person.

He *was* surprised by how friendly the people were, especially toward us. He was also surprised they called the War the "American War." The number of motorbikes was overwhelming, as was the way they got around on them and still survived.

According to Lou, the food was ok, but he was not impressed and did not trust it. One time, he had a chicken cockscomb in his phở. After I saw that I was not hungry, he said (I saw him fish that thing out of his soup, and couldn't really blame him).

Lou says he did not feel any type of closure regarding his war experiences because those experiences were limited, and he's forgotten a lot. He also said he only saw the villages during the War, and this time it was different areas. Although I do have PTSD, he said, after a pause.

Ray

Ray is glad he returned to Vietnam with our group, explaining that it was a combination vacation and sense of closure for him.

There were some difficult moments, including an incident during our visit to the Củ Chi Tunnel complex. When our guide demonstrated how the Cong set the various types of booby traps, it brought back bad memories. Although Ray never stepped in a trap during the War, he saw them, and saw what they did to people.

But Ray's most profound experience was our chance meeting with the North Vietnamese Army veterans. He was shocked when he first found out who they were but did not hesitate to join the line to shake their hands. None of them seemed hesitant to shake hands either, and Ray recalled different degrees of friendliness. Although none of them spoke English, our guide translated simple greetings and phrases.

After the encounter, Ray was shaken. He was thrown back to the time they were the bad guys. Then he was left wondering, did I just shake hands with one of the guys who was shooting at me, or was I shooting at him?

Ray had a nightmare that night. In the dream, the NVA vets pulled guns on them when they realized he and the vets were GIs. The dream ended, and Ray woke.

Ray theorized that the fact that the NVA vets were wearing uniforms contributed to the nightmare. Even considering the dream and his sense of unease, Ray no longer considers them the bad guys.

That's done, that's in the past, and I don't dwell on the past, he said.

The meeting was a bad experience for Ray at first, but later on, after he had some time to process it, there was perhaps a little healing. Even such a short meeting, Ray explained, made him realize they are the same as us in their thoughts, with the same hesitancies. It was an experience he's glad he had.

Kevin

The trip was like an explosion of experiences, said Kevin. He recalled an older lady we met in the Sài Gòn marketplace, how she spent 60 years running her stall. She relayed how people take care of each other's stands, reminding him of flea markets here. They create community, Kevin said.

Kevin recalled an odd story told to us by the father of a family we visited. The family had previously hosted a luncheon for American vets and their wives, including a surgeon who was asked to treat a severely wounded Việt Cộng soldier during the War. He was forced to amputate the soldier's arm, and took the arm home with him as a souvenir. Years later, the patient and surgeon were reunited during a visit, and the surgeon gave the former soldier back his mummified arm.

Kevin liked the new foods he ate on our trip. In the military you eat American food, he explained, so he never got the chance to really try Vietnamese food.

Kevin also enjoyed visiting Our Lady of La Vang Cathedral and retreat house. As a Roman Catholic, he loved learning about the pilgrims, and was amazed by the devotion of the Catholic population of Vietnam.

The unplanned meeting with the NVA veterans was a highlight for Kevin. He observed the apprehension on both sides at first, but once everyone shook hands, they started smiling, and there was a kind of breaking down of the walls. Kevin recalled how the conversation was limited but could sense by the eye contact and body language that they thought, *it's good to see you.*

The chance meeting gave Kevin a sense that the conflict was finally over. He has veterans in his therapy group who would never go, who hate the Vietnamese. They are still there, still living 50 years ago, he explained.

Kevin also relayed his and Mary's reflections after a seemingly everyday event at a coffee house in Sài Gòn. Several young women were playing a game similar to Parcheesi, and another came in with a baby. Kevin fondly recalled them all laughing, with everyone pitching in, taking care of the baby. Kevin said, you hear about and see how the young people work so much, but they still find time to get together with friends and family. The young people are not at war, so they can have leisure, have happiness. A large part of the population was not even born until after the War, he added.

I'm glad I went back, confirmed Kevin. There are some things in your life you have that are big questions and this helped to answer one of mine. Yes, we make a difference. Yes, the people are better off now. There were marketplaces back then, but they stunk so bad, were so dirty, no American would go near them. But now you see cleaner markets, you see their interactions with many international people. Vietnamese parents will do anything so their kids are educated. These are all positive changes, he said.

For Kevin, going back this time was like closing the circle—to see the whole country, to understand the mountains, the white beaches. Not just the bases and the poor villages.

It's a kind of closure, but not a closure like it's the end of things, he explained. It's like that particular point of my life is now over. You go through a lot of things like that in life, he concluded.

Ed

Today's Vietnam was pretty much what Ed expected because he did the recon mission and a lot of research before going. He knew it would be like visiting any place 50 years after its civil war.

What was impressive to him was how nice the people are and how there is virtually no violent crime. In the United States, there is theft, drugs, and murder in every city, he emphasized. They are brought up differently from us; they are very family-oriented. The dynamic reminded Ed of people in Italy. They were accommodating and pleasant to visitors, and not always just because they were getting money from us. They seemed to be genuinely nice to people as a default.

The driving conditions are crazy, and crossing the street in cities is scary. You would not want to drive there if you are used to traffic laws; you would get into an accident immediately. Ed added that he now understands why they do not rent cars without drivers.

Ed was impressed with the Khê Sanh Marine Base and Museum, and the War Remnants Museum in Sài Gòn, including their coverage of the Mỹ Lai massacre. While he noted the museums were slanted against the American side, he found this understandable since they considered us to be invaders of their country.

Ed loved the food and loved the low prices. Hà Nội was a fun city for him, especially Beer Street.

The chance meeting with the NVA was epic. They treated Ed with reverence upon learning he was a Marine. They wanted to touch him, keep shaking his hand, he recalled. Ed surmised they must have fought against Marines, and enjoyed the discourse with them. He noticed they were all fit and able to wear their old uniforms. I never had any resentment, he concluded. Resentment has no value.

Mary

Mary mainly traveled with us to support her husband Kevin, but she was also glad she joined the trip for herself. Although she did not serve in Vietnam, Mary is a Vietnam-era veteran, and the War has had a profound impact on her life. Mary has also befriended Vietnamese people throughout her life and was curious to see their homeland.

Visiting over fifty years after the War, Mary was amazed seeing the industrious Vietnamese selling anything and everything, trying to make a living, yet very friendly. Over the years, they have worked so hard, she stated admirably.

I think the trip was an absolute education, Mary relayed. The hatred back then was really towards the French, because they were the colonizers. The Vietnamese thought we wanted to colonize them too, but we were there to keep Russia from getting a port. The hatred for what the French had done to them translated onto us, she added.

Several other aspects about today's Vietnam stood out to Mary. The massive number of motorbikes and how they successfully weave between each other. The War is just a memory, yet Agent Orange destruction is still being felt, and sometimes addressed. The government exits if they need it, but it does not control them.

Mary said that dealing with the heat in Vietnam was the hardest part, and stressed how much water she and Kevin had to drink to stay hydrated.

As a dentist, Mary was curious how her industry operated in Vietnam. Trying to arrange visits through official channels did not work, as dental offices and clinics are all private businesses and not overseen by the government. Mary decided to walk into several Sài Gòn clinics at the end of the day when the staff were leaving, around 8:00 p.m., explaining where she was from and her interest. Each time, someone gave her a tour. She found all the clinics to be very modern, with state-of-the-art equipment and treatments. They employed polite and professional staff, with mostly female dentists who receive the same training as in the United States. Dentists she met in Vietnam work 12-hour shifts, six days a week, which is the country's standard.

Mary was informed that the young populace is very conscientious about dental hygiene and wants white, straight teeth. The clinics are paid by different insurance plans (including government insurance) as well as cash. People even travel from Australia to get quality work done at a good price, including implants and cosmetic procedures. Mary had heard it was like this, but was pleasantly surprised to see it for herself.

Author's Reflection

Although I am not a veteran, as the primary author of this book, I have included my personal reactions to Vietnam.

Visiting Vietnam was a real eye-opener for me, mostly because of what I *didn't* see. The Vietnamese lack anger, road rage, suspicion, and they are not defensive. They showed no animosity toward Americans or anyone else that I could see. Vietnam is an endlessly fascinating, picturesque country filled with often strikingly poor yet genuinely warm and happy people. Perhaps their temperament and psyche reflect their religions and philosophies. Maybe they don't require many possessions to be happy.

They appear to make the most of both socialism and capitalism, which seem to somehow successfully coexist. The government, although dysfunctional in many ways (as governments are, no matter the stripe), seems to provide a reasonable level of support without being overbearing. Since Vietnam is one of only five communist countries left, I was surprised to find that our guides and others we met spoke freely, and no one seemed paranoid or censored. Maybe they were just used to censorship and a lack of freedom of expression, but they did not appear remotely suppressed or bothered by it. As a visitor, I may have been seeing the best side of a face, and things may have looked different had I spent more time there.

Everything was available for sale, and they were incredibly industrious and entrepreneurial. Shortages did not seem to exist, and if they needed it to use or sell, they made it. Many are poor, but they all seem to eat, and all seem to have a livelihood (or two or three).

There's an amazing variety of fresh food available, both to buy and cook and to order in restaurants. You want phở for breakfast, schnitzel for lunch, fettuccine Bolognese for dinner? You can find all of it easily in any Vietnamese city, large town, and even some villages.

The freshness and variety of ingredients are overwhelming, in fact. The marketplaces are gems, with fair prices. They make creative use of everything, wasting nothing. Even people of lesser means, living in makeshift homes and wearing raggedy clothes, were shopping for fresh produce. No one I saw appeared malnourished. There were some fast food restaurants in large towns and cities, but they seemed to be patronized by trendy youth rather than providing affordable food staples for the poor.

Landscaped squares with the requisite monuments celebrating both the average communist citizen and party trailblazers were in every town. This was an exotic phenomenon for me, this hard-to-define, Brutalist-Soviet-throwback style with an Asian flair.

A few things bothered me. People throw trash everywhere, especially in the countryside. Younger people are less likely to do this, and the cities are starting to install trash cans, so things are moving in the right direction.

I was saddened to witness the use of slash-and-burn deforestation to make room for crops, with no regard for flora or animal habitat. We saw patches of burning jungle twice during our visit.

Where were all the birds, all the little wild animals? Unlike in the United States, I saw very few. It was eerie. Habitat loss, pollution, climate change, and illegal hunting and trafficking are all contributing factors. It made me appreciate our conservation laws even more.

While on the trip, Dad and I discussed Vietnamese drivers. They constantly cut each other off and beep their horns, yet they don't get mad. They seem to accept that this is the way of the road. Although people drive much more erratically than they do in the United States, we saw no road rage—no flipping the bird, shaking of fists, or catching up with someone to get even and cut them off too. Our discussion evolved into Vietnamese people in general, and how they just seem . . . calmer. Calmer than most Westerners, and certainly calmer than the super-hyped, on-the-go mentality of Americans. I could be wrong, but I suspect this is partially due to their Eastern faith and philosophical traditions.

Walking down any city street felt safe at all hours. In Vietnam there is little crime, and violent crime is rare. Hmm. Maybe it's because they are not always pissed off? I know what you're thinking: punishments are much harsher so that stops people from committing crime. But is that truly a successful deterrent? Most studies say no.

I admit I don't know much about the Vietnamese justice system. However, I can honestly state that Vietnamese people are not walking around in fear of the government. Not walking around in fear of getting caught or of getting punished. They are not walking around in fear of anything.

It's my personal opinion, of course, lacking peer-reviewed studies and data, but I believe that most Vietnamese people commit little to no crime because they are not afraid or angry.

Now, take Americans. We walk around in fear of getting mugged or shot in large towns or cities. In fear of getting ripped off or swindled. In fear of being lied to by politicians of all stripes. In fear of a virus, then in fear of a vaccine meant to curtail it. In fear of people not like us. Even children live in fear of an active shooter in their classrooms (and rightly so, as firearms are the largest killer of children in the United States). And yes, Americans even live in fear of other drivers cutting them off. Live in fear for so long and what happens? That's right, you get angry.

Americans are angry, and it seems to have gotten worse since the pandemic. My dad asked, where did we go wrong?

It gave me something to think about. And now, I've had plenty of time to form my personal hypotheses. I believe Americans are so angry because of three truths: the 24-hour news cycle, the ever-deepening political divide, and the increasing rift between the haves and have-nots.

Our for-profit news channels and websites sensationalize the news, have a political bent, and often lack journalistic integrity and proper fact-checking. There have always been bad people creating bad news, but now it's repeated to us all day, every day, and slanted to place blame on the "other side." Even seemingly innocuous stories are twisted so a finger can be pointed to stir up outrage. It's fear-mongering at its finest—and all for ratings.

Within the last thirty years or so, political issues have grown to encompass personal issues they did not previously—at least not to the current extent. Today, many politicians seem to have an opinion about what life choices everyone should make—ranging from healthcare to education. These are matters that used to be decided by experts in, well . . . the healthcare and education fields. The list continues, yet the point is that political forays into the realm of personal freedoms, sacred to Americans, have widened the divide. I seriously want to know . . . whatever happened to our national adage of MYOB?

And finally, the middle class is shrinking in America, and has been for some time, causing a growing chasm between the wealthy and the poor. Is it really a sustainable way to live when some families own multiple homes and cars while others take the bus to their three jobs, live in a roadside motel, and are one hospital visit away from bankruptcy? No one can deny that this disparity leads to resentment and hostility.

I've always thought that you learn the most about your own country when you leave it, not only by seeing other ways to live, but by gaining a different perspective and having a point of comparison. For instance, it was hard to acknowledge the overwhelming sense of fear and anger in my country until I was in a place where such fear and anger did not exist. All I can hope for is that more people in coming generations travel and observe life in other parts of the world, so they'll realize that there are other options for living.

Remarks from Our Vietnamese Planner and Guides

Our trip would not have been possible without the amazing planner who designed our itinerary and the guides who traveled with us.

Xuân Vũ Thành

Xuân Vũ Thành lives in Hà Nội and arranged our entire trip based on the various requests of my dad. Xuân says she tried to create an itinerary that allowed us to visit historical war sites that still remain, as many of them are now gone. She felt a bit nervous when planning a trip for American war veterans, as there may have been some sensitivities or apprehension among our travelers. Although she was born after the War and thinks the past is the past, she was aware that she had not lived the life of a soldier and could not fully understand how that might feel.

Xuân felt honored to be able to plan our visit and was happy to be asked for her feedback. She met all of us when we were in Hà Nội, and took my parents and me to dinner with her two young daughters. It was great getting to know Xuân, and I recommend her services at Asia Tour Advisor to anyone who visits Southeast Asia.

Thế Đăng Anh

Our northern guide was Thế Đăng Anh, a Hà Nội native. Despite the two Indochina wars in Vietnam, Thế always tells his tourists that he, like most Vietnamese, harbors no ill will toward Americans or the French.

He derives great pleasure from guiding American veterans, and speaks openly about the reality of history: that both American and Vietnamese committed wrongs, and no one can blame American veterans for the War. Thế remarked that both Vietnamese and American soldiers were victims of a proxy war, and could not determine the outcome. He praised our group of veteran travelers, especially the kindness, sensitivity, and flexibility of my dad during our challenging itinerary.

Anh-Cơ Nguyễn

Đà Nẵng resident Anh-Cơ Nguyễn was the guide for the central leg of our visit. Born during the American War, Anh-Cơ was very happy to guide our group of American veterans. Throughout his lifetime, including his tours for American vets, he's heard a number of stories about the War, both funny and heartbreaking.

Anh-Cơ's father was drafted as an Army of the Republic of Vietnam (ARVN) soldier in the American War. Like many draftees, he was unhappy about it, wanting to instead become a professor or a doctor. Anh-Cơ's background made him curious about the War's history, and despite encountering one-sided accounts, he tries to find the truth through reliable sources, specifically the first-hand memories of veterans. Anh-Cơ exclaims with enthusiasm: every day is a learning day!

Anh-Cơ most enjoys bringing American veterans to former battlefields. He says reactions to the sites vary, sometimes depending on whether the veterans were drafted or enlisted. However, he believes after seeing Vietnam on a peacetime return visit, many of them wonder: Vietnam is such a beautiful country, why did we come to fight in this place?

Anh-Cơ says he relished climbing Đồi A Bia (Hamburger Hill) with my dad and me. He explained that the hill is 937 meters (3,074 feet) above sea level, with about 1,000 steep and uneven steps leading to the top. The famous trek is a real challenge not only for visitors, but also for tour guides. After 50 minutes of effort, we reached the top of the hill, stayed there for 20 minutes to relax and look around, and then started to descend. It took us about two hours total.

Anh-Cơ said he was impressed that my baby-boomer dad was able to make the climb, and in such good time: Ed is still a rock in his late 70s. He is a Marine (once a Marine always a Marine), and he managed very well, but I still kept my eyes on his steps at all times, he recalled.

Anh-Cơ likes his English idioms and cheesy phrases, sharing many of them as our guide. During our climb, he spurred us on with a new, hokey encouragement, "A little care can get you there!" His jovial nature and our resulting laughter helped us to keep moving in the jungle heat.

The chance meeting with the NVA veterans was a pivotal moment for our veterans. Anh-Cơ thinks the meeting was a good experience for everyone, and wisely explained that both sets of veterans experienced the same fate in the War: they could have been killed at any time at a very young age, which is not what any of them wanted. Whether they became warriors by draft or volunteering, he knew they were all curious about their old foes.

Anh-Cơ said he has heard several times from both sides, "In war-time we were warrior enemies, now we are brothers." They don't hate, because time is the greatest healer for all. The War is part of both Vietnamese and U.S. history, and he firmly believes it is now the time for friendship.

By being a tour guide, Anh-Cơ has experienced how the aging process changes veterans. When they were 18-20 years old, they thought they were bulletproof, especially the volunteers, he said. After years of being fathers, grandfathers, and even great-grandfathers with many experiences in life, they often change their attitudes and thoughts about war.

I asked Anh-Cơ for his thoughts on America's involvement in his country's civil war. Anh-Cơ believes that the American War was a proxy war, or a war of attrition for all sides: the NVA (North Vietnamese Army), NLF (National Liberation Front), ARVN (Army of the Republic of Vietnam), and the U.S. military.

In Anh-Cơ's opinion, the United States was arrogant and didn't respect, study, or understand the situation or people of Vietnam very well. They relied too much on their toys, he said, and they couldn't improvise very well when they lacked supplies or support. They were like a bull in a china shop, and didn't take the advice of their ARVN and Aussie brothers.

Anh-Cơ believes that many U.S. soldiers didn't think of victory, only of the day they could head back home. These are the reasons he believes the U.S.A. couldn't win the War, why the NVA occupied Sài Gòn so quickly, and why Vietnam has been stuck between a rock and a hard place—or between a monster and the deep blue sea—since 1975 (I told you he likes his idioms).

The American presence in the War both helped and hurt Vietnam, Anh-Cơ said. The Second Indochina War caused immense damage, death, and family separation throughout the country. Yet, he added, the Americans also brought Western culture and opportunities via the democratic system of the Republic of Vietnam. And even though the South lost the War, as short-term American visitors in 2023, we recognized those subtle yet distinct differences between the North and South.

Thành Phạm

Our Southern guide was Thành Phạm, a man in his 20s for whom the War was only a chapter in a history book. Thanh's youthful politeness and soft-spoken demeanor seemed to embody everything about today's Vietnam. The young respect and honor their veterans and the elderly, yet have moved on from the wars and heartbreak of their past. They love Americans and the West, yet they have their own distinct culture and life philosophy.

Much like Thành himself, the future of Vietnam appears bright with advancement, opportunity, equality, and hope.

Part Four

Scorched Earth

Near the Vịnh Mốc Tunnel System, a U.S. bomb fragment from the War is still embedded in a large banyan tree over fifty years later.

I wish my head could forget what my eyes have seen.

–Dave Parnell

Agent Orange

Health Effects on American Veterans

All of the vets who traveled with us to Vietnam have PTSD. But they all also have physical conditions related to their service. In addition to combat wounds—such as Lou's injured hand and my Dad's leg—all of our vets suffer physical effects of Agent Orange.

Agent Orange was an herbicide used by the U.S. military during the Vietnam War, named for the orange stripe on its storage barrels. It was used between 1961-1971 to destroy dense trees and foliage in rainforests, wetlands, and croplands. Its use, which amounted to over 4.5 million acres, provided increased visibility of targets, revealed enemy troop concealment, and destroyed enemy food supplies.

A mixture of two chemical herbicides, 2,4-D and 2,4,5-T, Agent Orange and its manufacture created the highly toxic dioxin, 2,3,7,8-tetrachlorodibenzo-p-dioxin (TCDD). Dioxins are a group of chemically similar compounds that are persistent organic pollutants (POPs), meaning they don't break down easily and remain in the environment for a long time, often from decades to centuries, especially in soil and sediment.

The herbicide was usually sprayed from helicopters or from low-flying C-123 Provider aircraft, and fitted with sprayers, MC-1 Hourglass pump systems, and 1,000 U.S. gallon chemical tanks. Spray runs were also conducted from trucks, boats, and backpack sprayers.

All veterans who served in Vietnam suffered exposure risk. Those who flew on or worked on the C-123 aircraft, which were referred to as "spraybirds" (because they sprayed the herbicide), had the greatest exposure risk. These aircraft, contaminated with Agent

Orange residue, remained in the operational inventory even after the War, and some were later used for training by Air Force Reserves personnel.

Exposure to the dioxin contaminant in Agent Orange has caused serious health problems. The VA offers a free health exam for veterans and health benefits and disability compensation for those effected by Agent Orange, including dependent children.

The following conditions are currently recognized by the VA as "presumptive" for veterans exposed during service.

Cancers: Including bladder, prostate, lung, Hodgkin's, certain leukemias, and soft-tissue cancers.

Neurological conditions: Such as Parkinson's disease and early-onset peripheral neuropathy.

Other diseases: Type 2 diabetes, ischemic heart disease, hypertension, AL Amyloidosis.

Birth defects: Studies have shown a link between Agent Orange exposure and severe birth defects in offspring, including spina bifida, heart defects, neural tube defects, childhood cancers, behavioral disorders, and more.

Lasting Effects in Vietnam

The use of Agent Orange has left tangible, long-term impacts upon the Vietnamese people who live in Vietnam as well as those who fled in the mass exodus from 1978 to the early 1990s.

Recent corrective studies indicate that previous estimates of Agent Orange exposure were biased by government intervention and under-guessing. As a result, current estimates for dioxin release were almost double those previously predicted. U.S military data indicate that millions of Vietnamese people were directly sprayed during strategic Agent Orange use. According to the Vietnamese government, approximately 4.8 million Vietnamese people were exposed to Agent Orange and an estimated 400,000 Vietnamese people have died from cancers and other illnesses caused by the defoliant's dioxin. Beyond the fatalities, Agent Orange has caused widespread illnesses, birth defects, and continuing health issues. Levels of dioxin in the breast milk and blood of people in sprayed areas are still currently higher than in unexposed regions, indicating its potential to continue to affect future generations.

In addition to the human cost, the dioxin's environmental destruction has been unprecedented. Official U.S. military records listed the destruction of 20% of the jungles of South Vietnam, and from 20-50% of the mangrove forests, resulting in an overall reduction of plant and animal populations, soil nutrients, ecosystem productivity, and growth yields. The long-term effect of this deforestation continues to result in less-aged foliage and mangroves, with many patches of economically unviable grass colloquially referred to as "American grass."

Studies as recent as 2025 confirm that Dioxin TCDD is still entering the human food supply. Crops that were destroyed by Agent Orange produced an agricultural wasteland, with some farmers still confronting contaminated soil. Livestock has also been affected, as dioxins can be passed down the food chain via the fatty tissues of animals that are then ingested by humans.

Agent Orange and its toxic component, dioxin, are being removed through a multi-year, multi-million-dollar cleanup process by the U.S. and Vietnam governments. This process involves heating contaminated soil in large ovens to destroy dioxin at hot spots, as seen at the Đà Nẵng cleanup, and removing and safely disposing of contaminated sediment and soil at other locations, such as the Phù Cát Airbase. The cleanup of major hot spots, like the Biên Hòa Base, is ongoing and expected to take decades. However, recent cuts to USAID and other funding by the Trump Administration has left the future of the cleanup—along with other Vietnamese initiatives such as the clearing of bombs and explosives still left from the War—uncertain.

PTSD for FNGs

What is PTSD?

In the years following the Vietnam War, medical and mental health experts started delving deeper into the issues of stress in combat. What they came up with was post-traumatic stress disorder (PTSD), a condition derived from experiencing or witnessing extreme trauma. Severe anxiety and depression, violent memory flashbacks, hypervigilance, sustained drug abuse, and high rates of suicide were identified as leading symptoms.

In 1980, the American Psychiatric Association (APA) added PTSD to the third edition of its Diagnostic and Statistical Manual of Mental Disorders. Although controversial when first identified, the PTSD diagnosis has filled an important gap in psychiatric theory and practice. A study mandated by the U.S. Congress in 1983 surveyed Vietnam veterans and reported that 15% of men and 9% of women veterans were found to still have symptoms of PTSD, nearly a decade after the War was over.

In addition, PTSD sufferers are often plagued with physical conditions, including headaches, sleep disorders, memory lapses, continual pain, and gastrointestinal issues. Left untreated for long periods, it can even lead to chronic conditions like diabetes and heart disease. PTSD is often the root cause of emotional instability and substance abuse that in many cases has ruined relationships and hindered career advancement and even employability.

Compartmentalization

Many Vietnam veterans have been able to live productive lives with PTSD, often by using compartmentalization, a psychological defense mechanism that helped them survive the War. The tactic allows soldiers to cope with extreme and persistent stress caused by traumatic events and emotions by separating them from their everyday awareness. However, this short-term survival strategy, while working well in combat situations, often leads to long-term conditions after resuming civilian life.

In addition, compartmentalization rarely works as a long-term strategy for dealing with trauma. Suppressed memories resurface as flashbacks, nightmares, anxiety, emotional numbness, and disconnection, among other problems. While some Vietnam vets have used coping mechanisms that may have been adaptive and considered healthy, many were maladaptive and destructive. For instance, those who focused on jobs, family, productive hobbies, creative pursuits, sports, and other activities may have been more successful with long-term compartmentalization than those who focused on unhealthy relationships, secrecy and lying, avoidance, eating disorders, or drug or alcohol abuse.

While some veterans have lived their entire post-War lives practicing compartmentalization, be it adaptive or destructive, some have sought therapy, medication, and other treatments for their trauma. Even now, some elderly veterans are deciding to acknowledge and process their past, after finally receiving the acknowledgment and offers of assistance they have so long required.

The VA has also noted that some activities that align with getting older—such as retirement, health changes and reduction in alcohol use—can exacerbate PTSD symptoms or even trigger other war-related psychological stress. And although still a stigma in some circles, the good news is that overall, PTSD and other mental health challenges are no longer a taboo discussion topic.

Patient as Therapist

with Kevin Laughlin, EdD

Because of the uncertainties of a group of veterans returning to locations where they experienced multiple traumas, my dad decided it was prudent to bring a therapist on our trip. Kevin was the obvious choice, as he had already built a rapport and trusting relationships as therapist to some of our travelers. And of course, Kevin is a Vietnam War veteran himself. Being both a veteran and a therapist gives Kevin rare insights that I have incorporated into this section.

Because of the nature of those who served in Vietnam, some already had some form of Post-traumatic Stress Disorder (PTSD) from their childhood, Kevin explained. For many of them, the draft or enlistment was a way of escaping the family. Some also got into trouble with the law and were told to go into the service or face jail time.

Kevin explained how PTSD causes difficulty in all aspects of a person's life, including their career, marriage, and social settings and relationships. When Vietnam veterans returned home, PTSD was so debilitating that they picked up the bottle or drugs to self-medicate.

According to Kevin and many other sources, the VFWs did not initially welcome Vietnam vets, skipping a whole generation of warriors. Many of the World War II and Korean War veterans who ran the organization at the time did not think the Vietnam vets were in war long enough to be taken seriously. Many Vietnam vets who did attend were treated with indifference.

Research into the history of the VFW also shows that may Vietnam vets came home criticizing the War, therefore not aligning with the VFW's unwavering support of it. Some post leaders thought Vietnam vets were dangerous and unstable, and did not agree with their drug use. There was no formal policy against Vietnam vets, and leadership policy and debates within individual VFW posts varied. But the lukewarm welcome and lack of support from an organization that had been so vital to previous war veterans was yet another hurdle they had to face upon returning home.

When the American Psychological Society (APA) finally recognized PTSD as a distinct psychological disorder in 1980, it marked a significant step in acknowledging the long-term effects of trauma. Kevin explained that medical research revealed that sexually abused children and combat vets exhibited the same symptoms, including nightmares, trouble getting along with peers, and lack of success in school or employment. Many are chronically depressed and have generalized anxiety disorder (GAD).

Before it was officially recognized, many Vietnam War vets had already faced ruined marriages and careers due to PTSD. Some died by suicide, lacking the treatment and acknowledgment they needed. Many ended up homeless or in jail. Many were, and still are, apathetic that it has taken so long.

Although it took decades for advances in medicine and psychiatry, as well as legislative initiatives to change the system, the VA is now a crucially significant resource for Vietnam vets. But the military does not come and get you, even now, said Kevin. You have to figure that out for yourself.

There lies much of the challenge. First, vets need to be convinced that they have a problem. Often the spouse sends them to the VA, explained Kevin, but they also have to be self-sufficient, and must want help.

Those with PTSD usually do not suffer alone. Those who treat them often experience OTSD, or Ongoing Traumatic Stress Disorder. Essentially, this is chronic stress experienced by those caring for individuals with PTSD and other conditions. Those who suffer from OTSD are often overlooked, and include medical professionals and spouses and children of people with PTSD.

Spouses and children who care for PTSD sufferers rarely receive training. Going to the VA, getting treatment, having therapy, it's not just for the veteran, said Kevin, but for the entire family.

Veterans like Kevin who serve as therapists to other veterans face the dual obstacle of PTSD and OTSD. You think because they trained you to do the job and to be self-sufficient that your OTSD is temporary, he said. But it continues, just as the PTSD and the care continue.

PTSD and the Journey of an Infantry Marine

by Ed Woods

I separated from the Marine Corps in December 1967, out early for Christmas. I was recently married with a baby on the way. Separated they call it. I'm still not separated from the Marine Corps. I am hyper-vigilant, one of the symptoms of PTSD. To me, and others like me, it's a blessing. I sit at a table by the wall in restaurants. I know where the exits are. I see all the faces. Only then can I enjoy my meal and my company. In my reality, it just makes good sense.

For years I worked in a factory, usually night shift. I mostly worked alone, and no one bothered me as I did my job. Going out with the boys to the redneck bars after the 3 to 11 shifts occurred way too often. Bar fights and driving over the limit were my way of rolling the dice. I was putting a strain on my marriage and my family. I was ashamed. I left that job and developed a successful career as a professional photographer and writer. Charles, a Marine and the husband of Melanie, the woman who framed all of my artwork, asked me about my time in the infantry in Vietnam and insisted that I talk to a psychologist at the VA. I did, and was diagnosed with a 50% disability for PTSD.

PTSD has been around since people started throwing rocks and spears at each other. In the Civil War, it was known as nostalgia or soldier's heart. WWI combatants were shell-shocked and combat fatigue came about in WWII.

It's a plain but troubling fact that this world will always be barren of prolonged peace and armed conflict will inhabit the Earth till time eternal. Honorable service members will be caught in horrific situations not of their making, forced to do and see unimaginable acts that defy reason and comprehension.

I'm not a medical expert, just a patient. My observations are simply my experiences. My meds are working. I don't have many of the symptoms I endured before treatment. In the years following deployment to Vietnam, I was in denial. Nightmares, daytime flashbacks, hypervigilance, nervousness, irritability, headaches, and cold sweats were part of daily life. In the present, through therapy, medications and acceptance, I'm a good human. Nightmares are very infrequent. I deal with occasional flashbacks, embrace hypervigilance, and relate to fellow veterans. I sometimes imagine machine gun fire and look at the world through the sights of an M-14. I'm ok with that.

There is also something that the experts call triggers. A sound, a sight, or a scent that might trigger a memory. I have two. If I see an Asian man with a collared, short-sleeved white shirt, it brings back a very bad memory. If I smell meat burning on a grill, I immediately remember the aftermath of calling for napalm or white phosphorous to be dropped on enemy troops. Through therapy, the meds, and the support of my fellow veterans, I've learned to cope with these triggers. But like the hypervigilance and other symptoms, they are a part of who I am.

Understanding and Treating the Invisible Wounds of Service

by Patrick Sullivan, DO

Depression, anxiety, post-traumatic stress disorder (PTSD), and substance use disorders are among the most common and challenging mental health conditions affecting veterans. These aren't just clinical diagnoses, they are lived experiences that can quietly shape every aspect of a person's daily life, relationships, and sense of self or purpose.

Depression is far more than sadness. It is a persistent state of low mood, hopelessness, and loss of interest in life's joys. It can make simple tasks feel overwhelming, and can erode the connection a person feels to their family, friends, and even themselves.

Anxiety disorders cause a sense of constant worry, fear, or unease, sometimes so intense that it interferes with concentration, sleep, and physical health. For veterans, anxiety can be triggered by reminders of past trauma, or arise from the challenges of reintegrating into civilian life.

PTSD is a condition that develops after experiencing or witnessing life-threatening or horrifying events. For many veterans, combat trauma leaves invisible scars. PTSD can cause nightmares, flashbacks, hypervigilance, emotional numbness, and a sense of disconnection from the world. These symptoms aren't just reactions to the past, they can trap someone in a cycle where the trauma feels ever-present.

Substance use disorders often emerge as a way to cope with these overwhelming emotions and memories. Alcohol, opioids, marijuana, benzodiazepines and other substances may offer temporary relief, but over time they deepen the struggle and create new health risks, including dependence and addiction.

While these conditions can affect anyone, veterans are at a significantly higher risk. Military service factors such as prolonged stress, exposure to combat, moral injury (psychological distress from violating, witnessing, or failing to prevent acts that oppose one's core moral beliefs), physical pain, and the difficulty of transitioning home increase vulnerability. These burdens, carried in silence by so many, contribute to the heartbreaking reality of elevated suicide rates among veterans.

But while the challenges are real and often profound, so too is the hope. With compassionate care, the right therapies, and a focus on healing the whole person, mind and body, recovery is possible. Veterans deserve more than gratitude for their service; they deserve every tool and support we can offer to help them reclaim their lives.

How War and other Traumas Impact the Brain and Behavior, and Why It Matters

War exposes individuals to some of the most extreme and overwhelming experiences a human being can endure. Combat veterans may witness death, serious injury, destruction, and human suffering on a scale most civilians can't imagine. They may be forced to take lives in the line of duty, survive attacks or ambushes, lose close friends, or live with the constant fear that each moment could be their last.

These types of traumatic experiences can profoundly alter how the brain functions, not just emotionally, but neurologically. Understanding how this happens is key to recognizing that PTSD isn't a weakness, it's an injury, and one that can heal with proper care.

At the heart of PTSD is the brain's fight-or-flight response system, which is designed to help us survive danger. In a traumatic situation, under the influence of neurotransmitters such as epinephrine and norepinephrine, the brain's amygdala (our internal alarm system) becomes hyperactive, constantly scanning for threats. At the same time, areas like the prefrontal cortex (which is responsible for logic, decision-making, and calming the amygdala) often become less active. The hippocampus, which helps differentiate past from present and supports memory processing, in the presence of persistently elevated cortisol levels can also shrink or become dysregulated in people with chronic trauma exposure.

In war, (or persistent traumatic exposures for civilians) this heightened state of alert can persist for weeks or months, sometimes even years. For some veterans, the amygdala becomes permanently hyperactive, meaning the brain stays stuck in a constant state of high alert, even in situations that are objectively safe. This leads to hypervigilance, irritability, insomnia, and an exaggerated startle response—all common symptoms of PTSD. Loud noises, crowded spaces, or certain smells can trigger intense emotional and physical reactions. Nightmares, flashbacks, emotional numbing, and detachment from others are all common. This is not a sign of weakness or personal failure, it's a biological response to trauma that has rewired the brain's threat detection and stress response systems.

This rewiring of the brain is not imagined. It's real, measurable, and supported by brain scans and decades of neuroscience research. The good news is that the brain is capable of healing through a process called neuroplasticity, the ability to form new connections and pathways. With the right treatment, support, and lifestyle changes, the brain can begin to recover.

Today, we have tools that directly target these brain changes. Ketamine can reduce amygdala hyperactivity and support the growth of new neural connections. Transcranial Magnetic Stimulation (TMS) helps strengthen underactive areas like the prefrontal cortex. NAD+ infusions support cellular repair and energy production in the brain. Peptides can help reduce neuroinflammation and work synergistically with other treatments to increase BDNF (brain derived neurotropic factor). And psychotherapy, particularly trauma-informed approaches, can help individuals process their experiences in safe, structured ways.

Lifestyle changes also matter. Sleep, nutrition, exercise, mindfulness, and strong social connections can all help regulate the nervous system and support healing. These may seem simple, but they are foundational to long-term recovery.

When families and veterans understand that PTSD is not about "being weak," it's about the brain trying to survive the unsurvivable, it shifts the conversation. It invites empathy. And it creates space for real healing.

Veterans were heroes in war, whether they realize it or not. Not because they were unshaken by what they endured, but because they showed courage in the face of unimaginable circumstances. That same courage remains within them. If we can help heal these invisible wounds, many will go on to be heroes again. Not on the battlefield, but in their families, communities, and workplaces. With the right support, they have the strength not just to survive, but to lead, inspire, and continue making a powerful difference in the world, regardless of their age or whatever challenges they still may face.

There is hope. Recovery is possible. With the right care, the brain can change, and so can the future.

Why Veterans Are More Prone to Addictive Disorders

Addiction rarely occurs in a vacuum, it often takes root in the soil of pain, loss, and unhealed wounds. For many veterans, that pain includes the profound psychological and physical toll of military service.

Veterans are more vulnerable to developing substance use disorders for several interconnected reasons, and understanding these helps illuminate both the challenge and the path toward recovery.

First, unresolved trauma and chronic stress play a major role. Veterans are often exposed to repeated life-threatening situations, profound loss, and morally complex scenarios where every choice carries the potential for harm. Experiences that can leave deep emotional scars, along with lasting feelings of guilt or shame. When these wounds remain untreated, the emotional pain, hypervigilance, nightmares, and feelings of isolation can become overwhelming. In these moments, substances like alcohol, opioids, or sedatives may offer what feels like relief—temporary numbing of the mind or body.

Second, physical injuries and chronic pain are common after military service, especially for combat veterans. These injuries are often treated with medications like opioids, which can inadvertently lead to dependence. Pain and trauma together create a powerful force that can drive someone toward substance use, not out of weakness, but in a desperate attempt to function or feel better.

Many veterans do turn to self-medicating, rather than seeking professional treatment. There are many reasons for this. Some may feel stigma or shame about needing mental health care, believing they should be able to handle it on their own. Others may have had past experiences where they felt dismissed or misunderstood by the healthcare system. For many, there is simply a lack of awareness about the kinds of effective, respectful, and trauma-informed treatments that now exist—treatments that address both PTSD and addiction together, rather than treating one while ignoring the other.

But it's important to remember: self-medicating is a human response to suffering. The solution isn't judgment, it's creating pathways to real help, with care that honors veterans' experiences and provides safe, effective alternatives to substances. When addiction is seen not as a failure, but as a sign of unaddressed pain, we can begin the true work of healing.

The Overlooked Impact of Traumatic Brain Injury

Traumatic Brain Injury (TBI) is another invisible wound that affects many veterans, often going unrecognized or underdiagnosed. TBIs can result from direct blows to the head, blast exposures, falls, or rapid acceleration-deceleration events, all common in military environments. Even mild TBIs, sometimes referred to as concussions, can have lasting effects on brain function, especially when they occur repeatedly or are accompanied by psychological trauma.

The symptoms of TBI often overlap with, and can worsen, conditions like depression, anxiety, and PTSD. Veterans with a history of TBI may experience chronic headaches, sleep disturbances, memory and concentration problems, mood instability, and heightened irritability or impulsivity. These cognitive and emotional changes can alter a person's sense of self and strain their relationships, increasing feelings of frustration, shame, or isolation.

TBI can also contribute to personality changes that further complicate a veteran's ability to reintegrate into civilian life. A person who was once calm and reflective may now struggle with anger outbursts or reckless behavior. These shifts aren't a sign of weakness, they're the result of real neurological injury.

Faced with these overwhelming symptoms, many veterans turn to substances like alcohol, cannabis, or sedatives in an effort to self-soothe. They may drink to quiet the noise in their mind, use marijuana to fall asleep, or take pills to manage pain or anxiety. Unfortunately, what starts as self-medication, or even from being prescribed by a well-meaning physician, can evolve into dependence, and the cycle of suffering deepens.

Understanding the role of TBI is crucial in providing comprehensive care. Treatments must consider the full picture—physical, psychological, and neurological. Veterans dealing with both PTSD and TBI often need specialized, coordinated care that includes neurorehabilitation, trauma therapy, and support for cognitive and emotional regulation. With the right interventions, even the most complex wounds can begin to heal.

Can Revisiting a Site of Trauma Promote Healing?

The idea of returning to a place where trauma occurred, such as a battlefield, former deployment zone, or site of violence, is deeply personal and profoundly complex. For some veterans, revisiting these locations during peacetime can be part of a healing journey. For others, it may be destabilizing or retraumatizing. The impact depends entirely on the individual's current mental state, the support they receive, and the intention and preparation behind the visit.

From a psychological and neurological standpoint, returning to a trauma-related site can engage powerful emotional and memory systems in the brain, particularly the amygdala, hippocampus, and prefrontal cortex. These are the same areas affected by post-traumatic stress. In PTSD, traumatic memories are often "frozen" in the brain as fragmented, emotionally charged experiences that feel as if they're still happening. When a person revisits the site where those memories were formed, it may offer an opportunity to process and recontextualize the experience in a new, safer setting.

This process is known as memory reconsolidation, the brain's ability to update and reshape stored memories with new information. If done in a carefully supported way, revisiting the site may allow the brain to lay down new associations, such as a sense of peace, closure, or camaraderie, rather than fear or helplessness. This can, in some cases, lead to meaningful shifts in how the trauma is experienced and remembered.

However, this process is not without risk. For some, returning to the scene of trauma can trigger overwhelming distress, flashbacks, or emotional flooding, especially if the visit occurs without adequate preparation or support. That's why this kind of exposure should never be done impulsively or alone.

The most important factor in determining whether a return visit might be helpful is readiness. Veterans considering this step should ideally:

- Work with a trauma-informed therapist well in advance of the trip
- Clarify their goals for returning, whether it's finding closure, honoring a fallen comrade, or reclaiming a sense of safety
- Build coping tools and grounding techniques to manage distressing emotions if they arise
- Have a solid support system in place, either traveling with others who understand the experience or having regular check-ins with a mental health provider
- Plan time afterward for integration—reflection, rest, and processing any insights or emotions that surface during the visit

Healing is not about erasing the past, it's about reshaping how we carry it. For some veterans, returning to the place where pain was born may open the door to new narratives, renewed strength, and a sense of peace that had previously felt impossible. For others, healing may come in different forms, and that's okay.

There is no one right way to heal from trauma. But with preparation, intention, and support, many paths can lead forward.

Contingency Plans: The Case for Advanced Therapies

For veterans who feel they've tried everything—therapy, medications, coping strategies—and still struggle with depression, PTSD, or anxiety, there are advanced treatments that can offer real hope. In places like my practice, treatments such as ketamine infusion therapy (KIT), ketamine-assisted psychotherapy (KAP), intranasal Esketamine (Spravato), and transcranial magnetic stimulation (TMS) are used to help people move forward when other treatments haven't worked.

Ketamine Infusion Therapy (KIT)

Ketamine was originally developed over 50 years ago as an anesthetic, but over the past two decades, researchers have discovered its powerful antidepressant and antisuicidal effects. Unlike traditional antidepressants that may take many weeks to work (if they work at all), ketamine often begins to ease depression and suicidal thoughts within hours to days.

A low dose of ketamine is administered through an IV over a set period of time in a safe, monitored environment. Ketamine works differently from standard medications, helping to reset key brain circuits disrupted by chronic stress, trauma, or addiction. It also promotes neuroplasticity, the brain's ability to form new, healthier connections, which can support emotional healing and behavioral change.

While KIT is best known for treating depression, anxiety, and PTSD, it also shows growing promise in helping veterans struggling with addiction, particularly alcohol and opioid use disorders. Ketamine can help reduce cravings, interrupt compulsive patterns, and alleviate the depression, anxiety, and shame that often fuel relapse. For many, it creates a critical window of clarity and relief—helping them feel emotionally lighter, more present, and better able to engage in therapy and recovery. When used as part of a comprehensive treatment plan, KIT offers hope for those ready to break free from the grip of addiction and reclaim their lives.

Ketamine-Assisted Psychotherapy (KAP)

KAP combines the medical benefits of ketamine with the healing work of talk therapy. In this approach, a veteran receives a low dose of ketamine that creates a calm, slightly dissociated state, helping lower emotional defenses and quiet self-criticism. While in this state, they work with a skilled trauma therapist to process difficult memories or stuck patterns in a safe, supportive setting.

What makes KAP powerful is that it doesn't just reduce symptoms, it helps people make meaningful emotional breakthroughs. Veterans with PTSD often carry layers of pain, guilt, or shame that can feel too overwhelming to face. KAP helps create a space where healing those inner wounds feels possible.

Spravato (Esketamine Nasal Spray)

Spravato is an FDA-approved treatment for adults with treatment-resistant depression and for those struggling with major depression accompanied by suicidal thoughts. It is a form of esketamine—a molecule closely related to ketamine—and is delivered as a nasal spray in a medically supervised setting.

What sets Spravato apart is its ability to provide relief much faster than traditional antidepressants, often within hours or days. This can be life-changing for veterans who have felt trapped by depression or overwhelmed by suicidal thoughts. Spravato helps target and reset brain circuits involved in mood regulation and emotional processing, offering a new path forward for those who haven't responded to other treatments.

Spravato is typically used alongside an oral antidepressant, and treatments are given in a controlled environment where patients are monitored for safety during and after dosing. Like ketamine infusion therapy, Spravato offers hope and relief when it's most needed, helping to lift the weight of depression and reduce suicidal ideation so that healing can begin.

Transcranial Magnetic Stimulation (TMS)

TMS is a non-invasive, FDA-approved treatment that uses magnetic pulses to stimulate specific areas of the brain involved in mood regulation. It's most commonly used to treat depression, especially in people who haven't found relief with medication or therapy alone. TMS helps "wake up" underactive brain circuits, gradually lifting depression and improving energy, sleep, and emotional clarity—all without the systemic side effects of medication.

In addition to mood disorders, we also use TMS to treat neuropathic pain, including chronic headaches and migraines. By targeting brain regions involved in pain perception and modulation, TMS can help "reset" the way the brain processes pain signals. For some veterans, this means fewer flare-ups, reduced intensity of pain, or even long-term relief after multiple sessions.

Chronic pain and emotional suffering often go hand-in-hand, reinforcing each other in a cycle that can feel impossible to break. TMS offers a unique way to address both, reducing physical pain while also helping to stabilize mood and improve overall functioning. It's a safe, well-tolerated option that can make a meaningful difference for those living with the dual burden of depression and pain.

Each of these treatments offers hope to veterans who have felt trapped by depression, PTSD, pain or addiction. They are not meant to replace traditional supports like therapy, lifestyle changes, and community, but they can be powerful tools in a comprehensive, personalized plan for healing.

Choosing the Right Treatment: A Personal Decision for Veterans

When facing depression, PTSD, or other mental health challenges, it's natural to wonder: Which treatment is the best? The truth is, there is no one-size-fits-all answer. No single therapy—whether it's traditional antidepressants plus psychotherapy, ketamine infusion therapy, ketamine-assisted psychotherapy, electroconvulsive therapy (ECT), Spravato, psychedelics like MDMA or psilocybin, TMS or others—is universally "better" than the others. Each option has unique strengths, potential risks, and practical considerations. What matters most is finding the treatment that best fits each individual—their diagnosis, medical history, lifestyle, logistical and financial limitations, and goals for healing.

The first and most important step is a thorough medical and psychiatric evaluation by an experienced clinician. They should take time to understand the full picture, not just the primary diagnosis, and be aware of coexisting conditions such as anxiety, chronic pain, substance use, or sleep disturbances.

When Should a Veteran Seek Advanced Treatment Options?

Advanced therapies like ketamine infusion therapy, and ketamine-assisted psychotherapy are often recommended when more traditional treatments haven't provided enough relief. And some, such as Spravato and TMS, will only be covered by your insurance if you have not responded to two, three, or sometimes four different traditional antidepressants. But it's important to understand what that really means, and when it's the right time to consider these options.

These treatments may be considered for patients who have tried first-line therapies, such as antidepressant medications, basic psychotherapy, or other standard approaches, but still find themselves struggling. This is sometimes called treatment-resistant depression or treatment-refractory PTSD. It doesn't mean the person has failed, it means the treatments they've tried so far haven't addressed the full complexity of their condition.

For veterans, this can feel especially frustrating. Many have lived with their symptoms for years, tried multiple medications, seen several providers, and done their best to cope on their own. When the pain persists, it's time to explore other tools that can help reset the brain's response to trauma, break through emotional barriers, and provide real relief.

However, advanced treatments can also be appropriate earlier in the process for individuals with severe, disabling symptoms where rapid relief is urgently needed (such as suicidal thoughts), those who cannot tolerate standard medications due to side effects, and those who want an integrative, neuroscience-informed approach that addresses both the biological and psychological roots of their suffering.

Should Advanced Therapies Such as KIT Be More Accessible?

I strongly believe that advanced therapies like ketamine infusion therapy (KIT), and ketamine-assisted psychotherapy (KAP), should be more available and more commonly integrated alongside traditional treatments. These therapies are not experimental or fringe. They are evidence-based, safe when delivered by experienced clinicians, and in many cases, life-changing.

One reason I feel this so deeply is because of what I've witnessed firsthand. In my practice, I've seen so many patients, veterans and civilians alike, who have struggled for years with depression, PTSD, anxiety, OCD, pain or addiction despite trying multiple traditional treatments. They've taken medications, attended therapy, followed recommendations, and still felt trapped in their suffering. They come to the initial evaluation with a dread and fear that they "have tried everything" and have no hope left. When we introduced these advanced therapies as part of a comprehensive, personalized plan, I've seen remarkable transformations: not just in symptoms, but in hope, relationships, and quality of life. And in most cases, they had no idea these options even existed.

Ultimately, veterans deserve every safe and effective option we can provide, not as a last resort, but as part of a comprehensive, compassionate approach to healing.

When to Consider Advanced Therapies for Alcohol Use Disorder

Addiction, including Alcohol Use Disorder, is complex. It's not just about willpower, it's about brain chemistry, emotional pain, trauma, and sometimes physical dependence that can feel impossible to overcome alone. That's why I believe in using advanced, science-backed treatments like ketamine infusions, NAD+ infusions, oral medications, and psychotherapy together as part of a comprehensive plan. And yes, I firmly believe these options should be more available to patients everywhere, not just in specialized centers.

Veterans struggling with Alcohol Use Disorder may want to consider advanced therapies when they have tried traditional approaches (like counseling or 12-step programs) but are still struggling to stay sober; are dealing with co-occurring conditions, like depression, PTSD, or anxiety, that fuel their addiction; have intense cravings or withdrawal symptoms that make recovery feel out of reach; or are looking for more than just symptom management, but want to heal the root causes of their addiction

In my experience, combining ketamine and NAD+ infusions with supportive medications (like naltrexone or baclofen) and psychotherapy can be a breakthrough for patients who feel stuck. Ketamine can help reduce cravings, interrupt destructive patterns, and lift depression. NAD+ supports brain recovery at the cellular level, reduces withdrawal symptoms, and helps restore energy and clarity. Together, these treatments help patients feel stronger, more hopeful, and better able to engage in the hard work of recovery.

These treatments can change lives. I've seen patients who were trapped in cycles of relapse find freedom. I've seen people who felt hopeless rediscover purpose. These therapies aren't magic. Recovery still takes courage and commitment, but they give patients the tools they need to succeed. And in a world where alcohol use disorder claims so many lives, we need to offer every safe and effective tool we have.

Addiction is a neurobiological medical condition. Our treatments should reflect that, blending compassion, science, and personalized care at every step. If you or someone you love is struggling, don't wait until things feel unmanageable. The sooner you can find the right treatment and support, the greater the chance for lasting recovery and a renewed sense of life.

Why Some Are Hesitant to Try Advanced Therapies, and How That's Changing

Some veterans are understandably hesitant to try advanced therapies like ketamine infusion therapy (KIT), ketamine-assisted psychotherapy (KAP), Spravato, or TMS. This includes not only patients and families, but also members of the medical community. The most common reasons are stigma, misinformation, and simply fear of the unknown.

For patients, stigma can come from the lingering association of ketamine with its use as an anesthetic or with recreational misuse. Even though ketamine, Spravato, and TMS are safe and effective when delivered by experienced clinicians, that history can create hesitation. People may worry about how they'll be perceived for seeking these treatments, or wonder if it means they've somehow "failed" other options. But seeking help, and considering every tool available, is a sign of strength, not failure.

Misinformation plays a major role too. Despite the fact that these treatments have been studied for decades and are backed by science, many people (including some healthcare providers) still believe they are experimental or high-risk. In reality, hundreds of thousands of people have already been treated worldwide with IV ketamine, Spravato, and TMS for depression and PTSD, including veterans. Research and real-world data consistently show these therapies can provide life-changing relief, particularly for those who haven't responded to traditional care. In fact, more VA centers across the country are now offering IV ketamine and Spravato to veterans as part of their mental health programs, reflecting growing recognition of their value.

Other barriers include cost and insurance coverage, as some of these treatments aren't fully covered; cultural or generational beliefs, as many veterans come from backgrounds that emphasize self-reliance, making it harder to seek or accept help; and fear of trying something new, because when someone is already feeling vulnerable, the idea of an unfamiliar therapy can feel overwhelming.

Unfortunately, some in the medical community are also slow to embrace these treatments, preferring to stick with more familiar methods. But this is changing as more providers witness the benefits firsthand and as research continues to demonstrate safety and effectiveness.

The good news is that acceptance and availability of these therapies are growing every year. As stigma fades and education spreads, more veterans and civilians alike are gaining access to treatments that can truly make a difference. My hope is that we continue to break down these barriers so that every person who needs help can get it, without delay, judgment, or unnecessary struggle.

Final Thoughts

To every veteran and family member reading this: your pain is real, your story matters, and healing is possible. Trauma may leave scars, but it does not define who you are or dictate your future. With compassionate care, the right support, and evidence-based treatments, both traditional and emerging, lives can change.

In my practice, I have witnessed firsthand the power of resilience. I've seen hope return to people who thought they'd exhausted every option. Whether your path forward includes medication, therapy, innovative treatments like ketamine, psychedelics or TMS,

Collection boxes for dioxin victims such as this can be found throughout Vietnam. This one was inside a workshop we visited which employs disabled artisans.

lifestyle changes, or simply the courage to start a conversation, know that you are not alone.

Healing takes time, but it also takes hope. And hope begins with taking that first step.

Resources for Veterans and Families

U.S. Department of Veteran's Administration (VA)

The VA is the main provider of services and benefits for U.S. veterans. It offers resources for almost every area of veteran life, including compensation, loans, pensions, health care, employment, and education.

va.gov

General Assistance

Reach a live agent 24 hours a day, seven days a week or use the chatbot at **va.gov/contact-us/virtual-agent/**

1-800-MyVA411 or **800-698-2411**

Veterans Crisis Line, available 24/7

If you are a veteran in crisis or concerned about one, connect with caring, qualified responders for confidential help. Many are veterans themselves. You don't have to be enrolled in VA benefits of healthcare to connect.

Call 988 and press 1, text 838255, or **chat online at VeteransCrisisLine.net/Chat**

Other Nonprofit Veteran's Organizations

Many private organizations work alongside the VA to provide additional support and services.

Disabled American Veterans (DAV)

Provides free, professional assistance to veterans filing for disability and other benefits.

dav.org or **877- I Am A Vet (877-426-2838)**

Wounded Warrior Project

Offers programs and services for post-9/11 veterans with physical or mental injuries. **woundedwarriorproject.org** or **877-TEAM-WWP (877-832-6997)**

The American Legion

Provides support and advocacy for veterans, including help with benefits, employment, and community service.

legion.org or **800-433-3318**

Veterans of Foreign Wars (VFW)

Offers assistance with veterans' benefits, community support, and military advocacy.

vfw.org or **833-VFW-VETS (833-839-8387)**

Fisher House Foundation

Offers free lodging to military and veteran families so they can be close to a loved one during hospitalization.

fisherhouse.org or **(888) 294-8560**

National Resource Directory (NRD)

A comprehensive, searchable database of resources for service members, veterans, families, and caregivers, developed by the Departments of Defense, Labor, and Veterans Affairs.

nrd.gov

Military OneSource

A Department of Defense-funded program offering free consultations, coaching, and counseling for military families.

militaryonesource.mil or **800-342-9647**

Tragedy Assistance Program for Survivors (TAPS)

Offers comfort and care for anyone grieving the loss of a military loved one.

taps.org or **800-959-TAPS (8277)**

Vet Tix

Provides free or heavily discounted tickets to events for veterans and their families.

vettix.org

DAV Transportation Network

Operates a fleet of vehicles around the country to provide free medical transportation for ill and injured veterans.

dav.org

Inherited Scars

Being the child of a Vietnam vet means that your dad has a secret part of him that you never fully see. It's buried deep, but there's no denying it's there.

Sometimes it creeps to the surface and peeks out when the circumstances are right, like when he's calm and reflective and only around one or two trusted people. He may have had a drink or two, but not too many drinks because then he just gets angry.

He'll tell a brief story, something that seems unbelievable but you know is true. A story of his fellow soldiers getting shot around him as the bullets just missed him, or of enemies being thrown out of flying helicopters. When this happens, you've learned never to ask follow-up questions. You also can't act as shocked as you feel, but must keep your nonchalant face, like the one he carries.

If you succumb to wide-eyed surprise and desperate attempts at explanation, this will shut him down and it will be a long, long time before you see that secret part again . . . the part you dread but want to see because it helps you understand him.

These short snippets of his memory haunt you long after they are revealed. You can only imagine how much they have defined him. But each revelation, no matter how small, leads you a little further into the maze of his character.

Both my grandfathers were World War II vets. My mom's dad was an infantryman in both Europe and Africa, including the first-wave invasion on D-Day at Omaha Beach. My paternal grandfather endured more limited combat while building roads in Guadalcanal, Solomon Islands. There was a distinct difference in the demeanor of the two. My combat veteran grandfather also seemed to obscure a bit of himself, the way my father did. Of course, some of this has to do with personality and culture, but I've observed this among other combat vets of various wars. A part of them often seems vacant, although I know something is in there, buried or hiding.

I believe that governments steal something from children when their parent has been sent to war. A little bit of them is missing. The child senses this from a young age, but isn't always sure what the problem is. Spouses know. The veteran knows when he or she begins to uncover the traumas. Sometimes they learn to get it back, that buried part of them. Face the demons. Sometimes not.

My opinions and reactions to much in my life—war, history, politics, even family—stem from this background. Vietnam veterans hold a special place in my heart, and I am fortunate to have been able to interview, travel with, and get to know the veterans who star in this narrative. I am especially grateful and honored to have traveled to Vietnam with my father. I'll never completely understand what he has experienced in war. But I've began to learn the extent of it. The personal complexity.

Though certainly not without his wounds, both mental and physical, I feel that my dad was made stronger by his War experience. His character and resilience have not only remained intact, but grown stronger over the years. Sure, he's had his bad moments, drinking too much and acting grumpy. But being a combat Marine has also given my dad an existentially irreverent outlook about life and its challenges, which serves him well. Not in a disrespectful manner, but cheeky and carefree without taking any shit.

We are all a sum of our experiences, and when those experiences are profound and occur at an age prior to frontal cortex development, they can mold us dramatically. When he was a *teenager* (let's not forget that), the War put my dad in impossible positions, exposing him to moral dilemmas with no correct answer. He grew up fast, yes, but never lost his childlike wonder at the world around him. He holds it to this day in his late 70s, still delighting in new experiences, meeting new people, and visiting new places. He knows how horrible the world can be, and how self-serving people are, yet he roots for the underdog and always backs the good guys. And although this section is called "inherited scars," scars give us character. Scars tell our story. Yes, our scars have hurt us, they can be ugly, yet they should make us proud of what we have stared down and overcome.

People often say I'm like my dad. We do indeed have similar demeanors, similar senses of humor. And those personality traits were partially defined by his war experience. I inherited those too. And I am glad of it.

Part Five

Gathered Intelligence

Many young children help with family businesses in Vietnam.

Live as if you were to die tomorrow. Learn as if you were to live forever.

—Mahatma Gandhi

Tales of War and Beyond

When I began interviewing our veteran travelers for this book, I quickly realized that when asked to recall factual information about their military past, they were traveling back in time in their minds. So, in the middle of writing down military ranks and bases of operations, I was told war stories.

These stories are gold. A person can read fifty books about the military history of the Vietnam War, know the facts of each battle, the political positioning, and the long-range outcomes. But I believe these stories get you as close to being there as possible. I stood at rapt attention when hearing these deeply personal accounts. Some are shocking, some are hilarious. Most are heartbreaking. What they may do, dear reader, is get you a little closer to understanding these veterans whom I've grown so fond of and come to respect beyond compare.

Lou

Lou flew to Vietnam via a civilian 707 United jet, stopping in Guam. He was one of a group of rag-tag Army guys, all sloppy and wearing different uniforms. When Marines got off another C-141 military jet in starched uniforms and in formation, he was jealous.

While walking point one day—a role usually reserved for seasoned troops—Lou realized he was entering an abandoned North Vietnamese base camp. He just walked right into it. After discovering some graves, they dug them up and took a body count. The captain ultimately took credit for three dead bodies to meet his required quota.

Lou and a few others would sometimes drink at a small shack that sold beer to soldiers. On one such occasion, someone brought in a news article about the Kent State massacre. They had many questions, such as: why did the National Guard open fire? What did people back home know that we didn't? He will always remember this feeling of bewilderment and confusion.

Ray

When stationed at the combination Army-Air Force base in Long Bình, Ray was in charge of retrieving and storing all supplies for the officers' clubs. On each run, Ray was given an order listing the supplies he was to pick up at the Sài Gòn Navy base warehouse. The Vietnamese workers at the base (who did not speak English) would load more supplies than ordered, so he'd always have extra inventory. The items included various wartime delicacies, such as bottles of vodka, gin, whiskey, and scotch, as well as canned hams, produce, cases of beer and soda, frozen hamburgers, steaks, and French fries. Ray kept these extra supplies in a walk-in freezer under his control. Rather than selling the supplies on the black market, as many would have done, Ray decided to throw a barbecue on the base each weekend. He invited anyone who wanted to come for free food, booze, and camaraderie. Thirty to 40 people showed up each week, or whoever was off duty. Officers also came to Ray's barbecues and did not mind that he was using the extra supplies to provide a little R&R to the troops.

Ray was with the 554 engineers stationed at Bảo Lộc in the Central Highlands. There were four or five fuel bladders on the property, each containing JP4 jet propulsion fuel. The bladders were made of thick rubber, like big pillows, 30-40 feet square. One of the bladders was on a hill where the helicopters would land. It erupted, and the fuel ran down into a large pond owned by the postmaster of the nearby village. The fuel killed all the fish that were being raised for food. A claim was filed with the U.S. government, which provided the owner with a settlement for cleanup and replacement. Ray and his sergeant were sent to clean up the spill. Afterwards, the pond owner invited Ray, the sergeant, and an interpreter to a special dinner at his house in order to thank them. It was a more well-to-do home than most in the village. Ray enjoyed the different food and drink, including the main course of pigeon, a delicacy. No other family members ate with them, just the pond owner. Ray knew the dinner cost the man a lot of money, and he felt honored to be there.

Kevin

While Kevin was stationed at the 95th Evacuation Hospital in Đà Nẵng, six American soldiers took a helicopter to remove a North Vietnamese flag that had been tied to a tree with four ropes. The flag had been rigged with four Claymore mines, one on each rope. Kevin's face took on a ghostly look as he recalled the memory of their remains being brought back to the base, which caused a bad smell of death for several days.

Kevin served during the late stages of the War and observed the rampant illegal drug use among the troops. Marijuana use was widespread, while heroin use and addiction were huge problems. None of this was reported back to the politicians or people in the States. Soldiers were simply discharged and sent back home with drug addictions.

Not long after arriving in-country and being processed at Long Bình, Kevin was assigned guard duty for the day. While inside the shack, Kevin heard the screen door slam and looked over to see a soldier on heroin with a cut wrist and a .45 pistol. The soldier held the gun to Kevin's head and demanded a plane out of there. Kevin proceeded to pretend he was on the phone with air traffic, arranging a plane. He couldn't remember how long it was until someone arrived, put the man on the ground, and took his gun. Kevin relived this incident over and over in his nightmares, and the sound of the banging door later became a trigger for him. To this day, Kevin has no screen doors on his house.

The Vietnamese locals allowed soldiers to use their MPCs (Military Payment Certificates, used for on-base purchases) to buy drugs. The military kept changing the certificates to stop these black-market transfers, but the local dealers kept figuring out how to turn them into real money.

When Kevin was stationed in Đà Nẵng, the hospital was closed and moved to the air base 19 miles away. While clearing the wood and leveling the ground, Kevin discovered an underground cave with psychedelic paint on the walls, which people believed was an opium den used by the surgeons.

Kevin was posted to security and given a stack of small papers, each with a number from one to 36. He was told to report to a dirt road leading to the gate. Vietnamese girls, some quite young, were lined up and given the numbers, and the soldiers picked the number they wanted. Kevin told the chaplain and the captain that he was not doing it, not being a pimp. They told him he had to, because the overdoses, stabbings, and race riots on the base had slowed down since they started offering the girls. The base had gained a reputation for offering these services. It was 1972.

Kevin attempted to balance this negative interaction by delivering clothes to an orphanage and donating to a local Catholic church. He then began teaching English as a second language to a group of local Vietnamese people through the Vietnamese-American Association. A friend from that group invited him as an honored guest to his daughter's wedding. Kevin brought a Polaroid camera, which everyone loved.

The volunteer work was a way for Kevin to conquer his fears of this unknown culture and its people. These interactions and goodwill gestures also gave Kevin a rare insight into and understanding of the poverty and demeanor of the common people, something unknown to most American soldiers. Still, Kevin was apprehensive during his off-base outings because he never really knew which side someone was on, and he could get blown up at any time.

At one point, the Việt Cộng launched a rocket attack on his base, trying to hit a CIA listening device reported to be inside the hospital grounds. The ammo was locked up because of drug problems on the base. No one had the keys because the NCO and captain had gone into town to party for the night. Consequently, there was no ammo available to defend themselves. The troops had to stand up and pretend they had ammo in their weapons. Luckily, the bombing was all that happened.

Kevin was in the barracks smoking marijuana. A little later, he got a strange feeling and began to lose control, yelling and punching holes in the walls, all while the MPs laughed at him. Kevin found out later that the pot had been soaked in heroin because the dealers were trying to get people hooked. So many people were injecting heroin on the base that the garbage cans were piled with green syringe caps. Kevin stayed away from the pot after that and just stuck to drinking.

When his year was up, Kevin went back to Long Bình to process out, but his name never came up in the listings. Kevin was told to report to a room. A hairy arm came out and grabbed him, taking all his belongings—including his clothes—and he was put on a bunk. A doctor came in and asked how long he'd had a drug problem, because he had tested positive for morphine. Kevin said, I do not take drugs. He was put with all the drug addicts, including patients who were shooting up while the nurses played cards. Later, Kevin discovered that a doc had given him dysentery meds with morphine when he was ill. He never got back his belongings, including his medals and the contact information for all his friends.

Charles

During his first two weeks in-country, Charles took his first trip out of the area as part of a convoy. The truck in front was full of beer and hit a land mine. The driver blew out of the truck but was okay. Because they did not want to lose the beer, they simply replaced the track's cab. While this was happening, Charles watched jets dropping napalm fireballs in the distance.

Charles was sent to Củ Chi to retrieve the mail and could not return to Sài Gòn until they swept the road for bombs. There was a woman on the side of road, holding her little boy who had been killed by a truck. He had been decapitated, and she was trying to put his head and body back together.

While Charles was getting his allergy shot at the Củ Chi base infirmary, a little boy was brought in. Along the perimeter, someone turned a Claymore mine around, thinking the steel balls and shrapnel would shoot into the base. While the boy was playing, he set off the mine, blowing off half his arm. Charles is not sure if the boy survived.

Charles was riding shotgun on the way to get the mail. There was a jeep in front of them returning from the hospital. The jeep caught the bumper of an old truck and flipped into barbed wire on the side of the highway. Charles helped pull the soldiers out of the tangled barbed wire. Some of them did not make it.

During a rocket attack, two barbers who were hired to cut hair were shot dead on the fence by soldiers guarding the perimeter of the Michelin Plantation Base. It turned out they were Việt Cộng and no one knew it, and they were attempting to sneak back into the base for a night attack. If Charles recalls correctly, someone on the base had set a trip wire on the road, which allowed them to see the barbers before they got inside.

Inside the Michelin base, walking alone on the road to the PX, Charles spotted a wire. If he had tripped it, he would have been blown to pieces. It could have been set by anyone who came into the base, because you did not know who the enemy was. Even inside the base, roads always needed to be checked. You were never safe.

There was a Vietnamese laundry worker who had to sleep in a different place every night because the Việt Cộng would try to kill him. They didn't like that he was working for the Americans. Many Vietnamese workers had to hide for this reason.

Ed

On an early summer evening in 1965, Ed and his good friend Paul, both 19, were sitting on a bench behind Busty's Tavern in Upper Darby, Pennsylvania. Neither one of them had a girlfriend. Both had dead-end jobs but were taking night courses, Paul at St. Joseph's and Ed at the University of Pennsylvania, but they were boring classes in subjects like accounting and business law. They decided right then to join the Marine Corps as six-month reservists. It would transform them into men and keep them from being drafted and sent to Vietnam. The next morning, they signed up with the local recruiter, and a few days later boarded a bus loaded with other recruits for Parris Island, South Carolina.

On the way down, the recruits convinced the driver to make a pit stop at a roadside bar, so most of them arrived at Parris Island hung over, a fact not lost on the drill instructor. As they exited the bus, the instructor greeted them by delivering a hard punch in the stomach to the first recruit in line. During the 13 weeks of boot camp, Paul and Ed barely spoke, as the simple act of talking without being spoken to by a drill instructor was forbidden. Upon graduation, they were proud to be Marines and on their way to advanced infantry training at Camp Lejeune, North Carolina. The training was long and grueling, but Ed bought into the "gung-ho" Marine Corps attitude and excelled at all the infantry training. He was assigned the MOS (military occupational specialty) of 0311, an infantry rifleman—exactly what he had hoped for. Even though it was only for six months, he surely didn't want to be a cook or a mail clerk. He was an infantry Marine.

Near the end of his training, a captain talked about the war in Vietnam, and that many of them would be going, especially those with a combat MOS. He asked for volunteers to step forward. Not a Marine moved. The captain continued speaking. He spoke of "esprit de corps"—the feeling of pride, fellowship, and loyalty shared by a group—in this case, the U.S. Marines. The captain asked again. A single Marine stepped forward. Ed felt his feet move, and he stepped forward too. He wanted adventure. Paul was stunned. Ed was proud. He added two years to his enlistment, received a 30-day paid leave, and went home to inform his family.

During Ed's ninth month in-country while stationed at Phú Bài Marine combat base, he was told by one of the lieutenants that he was being considered for a promotion and would soon be in charge of his four-man fireteam. That meant more pay, so it was cause for celebration. At the time, things were a bit slow, with no attacks on the base for a while. So, although forbidden (the VC did not take kindly to villagers who were friendly with American troops), Ed and some friends bribed the guard and walked through the bush to a slopchute at the edge of a small village. They had a couple of beers, but they all felt on edge and headed back to the base. Their uneasiness came to fruition when two men with rifles appeared down the path. Both groups were surprised, and as the riflemen started running away, one of them threw what Ed thinks was a homemade stick grenade. The grenade landed pretty far away from Ed and his friends, so he didn't feel the impact at first. But a couple of small pieces of shrapnel landed in Ed's right lower leg and foot, and another Marine got a piece embedded in the web between his thumb and index finger.

Ed instructed the guys to keep it quiet, and they returned to the base. There was some blood, but they were able to apply small bandages. After a few days, all was well, except Ed's leg was not feeling quite right.

Someone had ratted on them, and Ed was called into the captain's office. The captain didn't seem too angry, but he sternly belittled Ed's actions: Woods, forget about that promotion, and be thankful I don't take a stripe. And go to sick bay for your leg. As a punishment, Ed was assigned "office hours," which is the Marine Corps way of saying nonjudicial punishment (Article 15) for a minor infraction, but this never materialized.

Ed's leg was a bit swollen and leaking from the cuts, so the corpsman in charge of sick bay sent him to the field hospital on the base. He was informed that his leg was infected and that they could not treat it, so he was being medevacked to Clark Air Force Base in the Philippines.

Ed wasn't happy about it, and he's still not. Ed says he made a mistake and put his fellow Marines in unnecessary peril. But his buds were happy for him. They arrived in the 'Nam together, and were about two months or so from freedom. Ed's chopper ride to Đà Nẵng airport was filled with both sorrow and elation. He was happy to be headed home, but sad to leave his Marine buddies. He was hearing those Huey rotors for the last time.

The plane ride in a C-130 to Clark Air Force Base was filled with injured soldiers, Marines, and the moans of pain and suffering. Once they arrived, everyone was lined up on gurneys or in wheelchairs on a dusty tarmac, squinting at the roasting sun. Ed's leg was severely swollen and painful. An airman with a clipboard and a pen, along with a doctor in full uniform, was moving from patient to patient. The doctor quickly evaluated each man.

They arrived at Ed's stretcher, and without looking at anything but his leg, the doctor pronounced: Take it off below the knee.

NO, NO, Ed shouted, raising hell. I'm not an Army guy! I'm a Marine! Again, not looking at the troubled human below him, the doctor calmly uttered: Send him to Yokosuka.

A few hours later, Ed arrived at the Yokosuka Naval Hospital in Japan where they informed him that he'd be there for a while, but leaving with his leg. Ed was good with that. The doctors performed multiple skin grafts over three months, and on one occasion, a nice nurse took him in a wheelchair to see Mt. Fuji. Ed was then on his way to the Philadelphia Naval Hospital with a scarred but otherwise perfectly intact leg. Semper Fi.

⌖

While fulfilling his time commitment back at Camp Lejeune, Ed was often able to leave on weekends. Camp Lejeune is a very large military base with countless troops from many different states. With true Marine Corps ingenuity, someone created a central area that could be used on Fridays as a meeting place for Marines who had "liberty." You could meet with drivers and other passengers going to different areas of different states. Ed would seek out a driver with a Philadelphia or South Jersey destination poster, and when the driver had enough passengers to fill the vehicle, they would all negotiate the cost. This process of leaving for weekend liberty was called "swooping."

Hey Ed, are you going to 'swoop' this weekend? I'm driving to Philly!

So, one fine Friday, they crammed five guys into a driver's car—three going to Philly, and two headed for South Jersey. After releasing the Philly guys, they headed across the bridge.

What towns are you guys going to? They both said Glassboro. Upon entering the town, what street, jarheads? Oakwood Avenue, Ed answered.

Hey, I'm going to Oakwood Avenue, said his now nervous fellow traveler. Back in the 60's, Oakwood Avenue was a country street with few houses.

What street number, he asked? 306, said Ed.

You're going to my girlfriend's house, you're going to my girlfriend's house! How could she do this to me, the other Marine yelled frantically.

They arrived at 306 and exited the car. Ed's fellow passenger, the supposed jilted lover, saw his girlfriend come out of her house—at 304. His girlfriend lived next door to Ed's. What were the odds?

After Ed was injured and finished with his hospital stay, he was sent to Camp Lejeune to spend his last couple of months and fulfill his time commitment. They did not know what to do with him, so he and two other guys were assigned to guard the armory. They also picked up trash with a long stick with a nail on the end. Ed says it was the best military job he ever had. He never even had a uniform during this time. But two days before he was set to be discharged, an officer asked, where is your uniform? Ed said he had never gotten one, and was told that he could not get out without a uniform. On his last day, he finally got the uniform so he could be discharged.

Veterans' Personal Observations on the War

Lou

According to Lou, our involvement did not help the Vietnamese. He believes, like many, that America's contribution was negative and political. He added that the War was not a mistake, but that it was not handled properly. He thinks we could have won if Nixon had not been afraid of pissing off the Russians.

He then stated one of the most common phrases I hear from veterans: That's the problem with politicians running wars.

Lou suggests that anyone who wants to learn more read Tim O'Brien's *The Things They Carried* and *Lone Survivor* by Marcus Luttrell.

Charles

The Vietnamese people did not want us there during the War, Charles said confidently. We were supposed to be helping them, but it was easy to realize they did not want us there. Furthermore, he doesn't think the U.S. military did any good while there. Charles recalls that during the War, some soldiers asked, what are we here for? Our plan did not work, he said, so yes, he thinks it was a mistake—similar to the U.S. actions in Afghanistan and the instability caused by removing Saddam Hussein in Iraq.

The Vietnamese people woke up and figured out they followed the wrong dog, said Charles, and now they realize the way to go is what they are doing now. He opined that the situation changed because the Russians imploded, not because the U.S. was there for the better.

Charles said he's curious why the U.S. government is now cleaning up the central/DMZ areas of Vietnam and footing the bill. He thinks maybe the U.S. will put an Air Force base there? He believes that if the Vietnamese government asked, we would do just that. In the future, Charles thinks the Vietnamese economy is going to skyrocket if the Chinese government does not interfere.

Ray

Ray believes that America's military intervention had no lasting impact on Vietnam. Fifty-some years later, he said, they are still the same people, though Sài Gòn has become more industrialized. They are still poor overall and still wear pointy hats. Despite it all, they seem happy, he concluded.

Kevin

Kevin felt sorry for the South Vietnamese when everything collapsed in 1975 and their system was overthrown after Sài Gòn fell. He remembered people hanging on helicopters trying to get out, especially the Amerasian children. Years later, Kevin met a Vietnamese boat person—a Catholic priest—who gave him a first-hand account of his escape.

Yet, after much reflection and a return visit, Kevin believes the American military made a positive difference overall. During the War, they thought we were trying to steal their country like the French did when they colonized Vietnam, he noted. They love Americans now, and they enjoy some freedoms. They realize they were lied to, the same way our government lied to us. Governments lie to people and keep us from being friends, human being to human being, he concluded.

Ed

By Ed Woods

Late summer, 1964. Two U.S. destroyers stationed in the Gulf of Tonkin in Vietnam radioed that North Vietnamese forces had fired upon them. In response to these reported incidents, President Lyndon B. Johnson requested permission from the U.S. Congress to increase the U.S. military presence in Indochina. On August 7,

1964, Congress passed the Gulf of Tonkin Resolution, authorizing President Johnson to take any measures he believed were necessary to retaliate and to promote the maintenance of international peace and security in Southeast Asia. This resolution became the legal basis for the Johnson and Nixon administrations' prosecution of the Vietnam War.

Politicians start wars, and young people fight wars. I was one of the young men who arrived in the spring of 1965 with other Marines as part of the first combat troop deployments of the War.

To this day, I am not a person who will analyze the whys and the reasons for America's involvement that took the lives of more than 58,000 of my brothers and sisters.

Unpleasant memories of my deployment haunt me. Yet, having served as an American in Vietnam makes me proud. I cannot analyze whether or not America's involvement was good for the country of Vietnam. It wasn't good for America.

Mary

At the time, Mary said, Americans were forced and drafted into the conflict. It was a very profound event, the War. It changed all our lives and dominated everything for so long, and the soldiers coming home were treated so badly because it had dragged on for so long. But they just had to get jobs and get back into society; there was no choice, she confirmed.

There are so many different factions of Vietnam—different tribes, clothing, and houses, Mary continued. Our recent visit helped Kevin connect it all and put the puzzle together, especially meeting the NVA veterans.

When in the military, you are just told what to do, and there were harsh conditions. Kevin wanted to learn about the people there because he is curious person. He's not the type to just follow orders; he is a questioner, she explained. Now he has the whole picture, she concluded.

Letters Home

These two letters written by Ed Woods to his family appeared on the front page of *The News of Delaware County.* They include personal messages, but also relay the confusion experienced by combat troops who were not always immediately aware of the military strategy.

May 19 (I think)

Dear People

Hi its me, PFC E J Woods Jr

How is everyone? I'm sorry I haven't been writing but I was stuck in a foxhole for the last 3 days. Somebody has been shooting at us. Not attacking, but shooting from long range. We don't even know who it was. The Vietnamese Marines are fighting the Vietnamese Army the Buddhists are fighting the Catholics and somebody is fighting the I Corps, another Vietnamese military branch. We don't know who we're fighting; it could be anyone of them or the V.C. The political situation is so messed up nobody knows what they're doing.

When they were shooting at us, we had some sailors here. One of them went crazy. He kept saying "I'm only 22, I'm too young to die." He was crying all over

PFC Edw J. Woods
III Marine Amph Force
c/o FPO San Francisco - Calif 96602

Home Address 7943 Arlington Ave Upr Darby, Pa.

the place." The captain hit him on the head with his pistol to shut him up so he wouldn't give us all away. I've got a soft head so I don't any when they shoot at me. I just crawl inside of my helmet and smoke cigarettes.

All the stuff that you send doesn't get ruined. Only the jelly-babies got ants in them. Nothing else got messed up. Over here ~~they're~~ there aren't that many ants, anyhow.

No I'm not going on any patrols over here, now, there, I answered that one.

Hey, Mom, that picture you sent me looks good. You look skinnier. Honey your hair looks really good. You look almost good enough for me if you weren't my sister. Almost I said. You and Ree Ree had better write them guys. Don't worry, you'll never meet them probably.

I missed a lot of sleep the

last few days. And I didn't write any letters for four days. Of course it rained in my nice dry foxhole. When it rains here it really rains. It comes down so hard you can't see a foot in front of you.

I think I still have that cold I caught up in Canada. Hey Mom remember I called you from there. You thought I was calling from New York when you took the call. "Hey mom, guess where I am, Montreal." That was funny. Until the car busted.

I guess school will be getting out about a week or so after you get this letter. I remember the summers well. I used to go down the shore and then I'd call collect again. Only then I'd say; "Hey Mom guess where I am Ocean City." The next time I call I'll say, "Hey Mom, or Dad, or Honey Ree Ree, Jeanie, or Joanie, guess where I am, Bangkok or Hong Kong or Tokyo, or somewhere. That'll be the collect call of them all. I think now I'd better call someone to give me a light and a can of oil so I can clean my rifle. I'll sign off for now.

Wy it's an hour earlier than I thought. I'll write some more

Misery is finding a rat in your foxhole.
Happiness is March 1969
Misery is wet sand in your skivvies.
Happiness is canned peaches for chow.
Misery is liver for chow.
Happiness is getting mail from home
Misery is insects
Happiness is R&R.
Misery is not knowing who is trying to kill you. (so is frustration)
Happiness is having so many people praying for you

Misery is running out of soap
Happiness is finding a new bunch of comic books at the P.X.
Maturity is realizing (finally) that life isn't one long weekend.
How do you like my literary masterpiece?
Now it really is time to go. Bye for now.

Love
Eddie

P.S. Don't worry about me, see how high my morale is.

This is specifically relayed in the second letter where Ed believed the "good guys" were attacking, when in reality, ARVN planes were firing on VC troops who had infiltrated the U.S. Marine base. *From the collection of the Historical Society of Pennsylvania.*

May 21st

Dear Mom + Dad,

Things are bad now. This is what I've been waiting for and afraid of since I got here. We were hit by planes and tanks and 50's. Not from the VC. From the Vietnamese Army. They dropped tear gas on us. It was heavy in the air for about 5 minutes. It seemed like an eternity. No gas masks. Dad, I guess you know what even 10 seconds of tear gas is like. That wasn't the worst. Sgt. Wojcik lost both his legs when a tank round landed next to him. Holdt caught it in the neck. He's dead. If the people who we are trying to help are killing our people, why am I here.

The planes won't come back. The tanks might. I don't feel too good. I hope it gets to the papers back home. Maybe it will make the people back home mad enough to do something. Say your prayers now.

Love

Eddie

A Letter to the People of Vietnam

by Ed Woods

I'll be 80 years old this year, and I plan to keep going for as long as I can. At age 19, I spent nine months and 18 days in Vietnam as a United States Marine infantryman in what you call the American War. It's a short amount of time in a relatively long life, but your country became a part of me during that time.

Most of you are too young to have lived through that war, learning about it only in your history classes or from stories told by older relatives. But you probably know that most combat troops experience trauma, and that trauma transforms people. It seems to mark us for life.

You were probably also taught that many of your people were my enemy when I was an American combatant, and some were my allies. Often, it was hard for us Americans to tell.

It was a journey fraught with horror, adventure, and tragedy. I first met a curious young local girl named Mai when my company of Marines arrived at our base in Đà Nẵng. She was drawn to me because of the red hair on my arms and under my cover (that's Marine Corps speak for hat). She had never seen a person with red hair in all of her five years.

In 1965, the base consisted of a few small guardhouses at the corners, with walls of endless coils of concertina, or razor wire. There were semi-permanent structures for the command center, a field hospital, and a mess hall. Our company was housed in tents with temporary wooden floors, four Marines to a tent. This is how I lived.

Mai lived in a village hut on the edge of the jungle with her family. I never went there, but I saw other places like it. People lived simply yet seemed easygoing, despite the ongoing war.

Our infantry company's main assignment was standing guard at the various entrances, or patrolling the jungle and adjacent hills, to keep the enemy from getting close enough to initiate mortar fire on the base. Those patrols were usually one or two overnights. It was a gift to pull guard duty.

Whenever I went on patrol, Mai would wave to us as we left the compound. Upon our return, she would be there with a hug. If the night before had been filled with the sound of explosions and small arms fire, the hugs were longer and tighter.

Despite the differences, Mai reminded me of kids back home: my sisters when they were younger, my cousins, my neighbors. Halfway around the world, surrounded by the enemy–I realized we are really all the same when it comes down to it. Children are curious, friendly, and trusting, until they are taught not to be. They fear for themselves and their families in the face of violence. It doesn't matter what they look like, what type of home they come from, or what language they speak.

In retrospect, I don't know if my country did any good in yours, or if it was all a mistake. For a Marine in the bush, there is no room for sentiment. We could debate that for days and still not come to a definitive answer. But I'm not here to discuss politics; that's for the politicians. Unfortunately, they think conducting wars is for them, too.

A couple of years ago, I came back to your country to visit—first with my son, and then with my wife, daughter, and a small group of other American veterans. Although we visited former war sites, we also saw your country as tourists: sampling your food, befriending locals, and enjoying your bustling cities and breathtaking countryside. These were things I never really got to do all those years ago as an infantryman.

At the Huế Citadel, our group met some of your veterans who fought against us, whom we called North Vietnamese, or NVA soldiers. We shook hands and posed for photos; it was kind of surreal. Like Mai all those years ago, they reminded me how we are all the same, despite our place on the map or our form of government. Those veteran heroes of yours were our former enemies, yet now they are grandpas, just like us, hoping for the best future for their grandkids.

Going back to Vietnam 58 years later was kind of like "closing the circle," as they say—putting some things to rest, maybe; some bad stuff, at least partially. Some traumas will never go away, but therapy has taught me why. Good people put in impossible positions do bad things in war. There's no way around that. Understanding this is key to acceptance. And sometimes, extreme challenges can even make us stronger.

In 1965-66, it was imperative for American Marines not to trust any Vietnamese adults, male or female. We could not tell a Việt Cộng combatant from a civilian. The ARVNs (Army of the Republic of Vietnam) were our allies, but out of an abundance of caution, we could never fully trust them, either. When we passed through a village, we saw women, children, and very old men. We learned to assume the missing men were either ARVN allies or Việt Cộng enemies. The only Vietnamese friend I ever had was Mai.

With the exception of my friend Mai, I do not recall the beauty of your country or the warmth of your people from my initial visit as a young Marine. My mission and the circumstances disallowed that kind of vision or humanity. However, during my two recent visits, I was free and privileged to develop friendships and interact with the people of Vietnam. My friend Xuan arranged our itineraries in the North, Central, and South. She visited my son and me in Hà Nội on my first return to your country, and on my second return visit, she and her two young daughters escorted my wife, daughter, and me to an awesome traditional dinner at a local restaurant. In true Vietnamese style, Xuan and her daughters arrived at

Ed and his friend Mai at the Marine Corps base in Đà Nẵng in 1966. Mai's father worked on the base, and she would come with him to visit her favorite American and tousle his red hair.

our meeting place on a small motorbike, with one girl sitting on the front fender, and one on the seat behind her mom.

It was also a privilege to befriend the three guides who escorted us around your country. I still keep in touch with Thế, Anh-Cơ, and Thành, and truly hope we can all meet up again someday.

On my recent two journeys to Vietnam, I sought to learn all about your country, cuisine, culture, and people. Crime, I was also told, is mostly petty theft, and violent crime is extremely rare; harsh penalties including the death penalty await the perpetrators. Illicit drugs are sometimes problematic, mostly in cities. Again, harsh penalties, including lengthy prison terms, limit these activities.

I also hypothesize that crime is low in your country for other reasons. I was told that homelessness is unusual, and that if homeless folks are encountered, the government finds a place for them to live. Yet most strikingly, most of you seem generally happy, at ease, and unafraid—certainly strong deterrents to a life of crime.

Your form of government differs from mine, and both have their positives and negatives. But one thing I noticed is that your government often seems to serve its people. For example, while traveling through Hà Nội one afternoon on our tour bus, we saw several barbers cutting hair in an area by the side of the road. I was told that once a week, free haircuts are offered and paid for by the government. Nice.

At several highway rest stops, I encountered people under tents, usually young women, sitting side-by-side at large tables painting and producing small works of art (one hangs in my home as I type these words). The table coverings usually didn't reach the floor, so I could sometimes see the artists' deformed feet or lower legs. I was told that the government keeps many disabled people employed this way. The conditions of many of these people are a direct result of Agent Orange, the chemical compound used by the American government to destroy vegetation and serve the purpose of war.

To this day, Agent Orange still poisons your civilians as well as many American military men and women who served in Vietnam, like me. Currently, I am in recovery after battling prostate cancer for two and a half years—a condition presumptive to Agent Orange

Xuân and her two daughters pose with Ed, Fran, and Colleen after a traditional dinner in Hà Nội in 2023.

exposure. It took a long time, but my government has acknowledged it, and is now taking care of me, too.

In closing, I want to thank the people of your country. I learned immensely during my two recent visits. The friendliness and courtesy of the people I encountered were unmatched in my many travels.

I arrived in your country as a 19-year-old boy from Eastern Pennsylvania who doubted he would ever make 21. Your country remains a formative factor in my life. I suffered much from the complexities of war, and upon my return visits, I learned much from both the strangers I met and the friends that I gained.

Some of it was tragic, and some of it was magic. Thank you, Vietnam.

Ed Woods, USMC
February 2026

Glossary of Terms

A

Agent Orange: A toxic herbicide and defoliant mixture used by the U.S. military in Vietnam from 1961-1971 during Operation Ranch Hand. Produced primarily by Monsanto and DOW Chemical, it was used to defoliate forests, destroy crops, and clear vegetation in order to remove enemy cover and food supplies. It's known for its harmful health effects on those exposed, including Vietnam veterans and civilians in Southeast Asia. The name comes from the orange-colored stripes on the 55-gallon storage drums used to store the chemical. Exposure to Agent Orange has been linked to numerous health problems, including various cancers, Type 2 diabetes, hypothyroidism, and birth defects.

Amerasian: A person of mixed American and Asian heritage, specifically referring to children of Vietnamese women and American soldiers during the War. In Vietnam, these children often faced social stigma and were sometimes referred to as bụi đời (meaning "children of the dust," since they were often wanderers or lived in the streets).

Ancestor Worship or Ancestor Veneration: A cultural practice of families honoring deceased relatives believed to influence the living. Maintaining altars and shrines with offerings to ancestors is common in Vietnam and stems from the core Confucian value of filial piety and family continuity.

Arc Light: The code name for B-52 Stratofortress strikes. These operations shook the Earth for ten miles away from the target area. The B-52 would often drop 500 lb. bombs from a 30,000' altitude that would hit in a row up to 100 yards long, often referred to as "carpet bombing."

ARVN: An acronym for **Army of the Republic of (South) Vietnam**, also **SVA (South Vietnamese Army)**, the primary U.S. allies during the War.

B

Benzodiazepines (or benzos): Central nervous system depressants that slow brain activity. They were sometimes prescribed to U.S. troops during the War to treat extreme stress, anxiety, and insomnia.

BLUF: An acronym for **Bottom Line Up Front**. A military communication strategy of relaying the most important information first rather than building up to the point.

Bodhisattva: In Mahayana Buddhism, a person who has attained enlightenment but delays entering Nirvana to help all sentient beings reach awakening. They are viewed as selfless guides who embody compassion.

Boondoggle: A term used to describe an operation that is absurd or useless, or not completely thought out.

Boonies: The jungle or any remote rural area outside of a base.

Boot: A term primarily used by Marines to describe a new soldier in Vietnam fresh from the United States. Also called a "cherry," "newbie," or "FNG."

Bouncing Betty: Nickname for a type of bounding mine or explosive device that, when tripped, launches into the air before detonating.

Brutalism: A mid-20th-century architectural and artistic style known for large blocky forms, raw concrete, exposed structures, and utilitarian characteristics. Emphasizing function and material honesty over ornamentation, it was born from post-World War II needs for strong yet affordable construction.

Buddhism: A spiritual tradition and philosophy aimed at liberating individuals from suffering by embracing the reality of impermanence and achieving enlightenment. Through meditation, ethical living, and understanding karmic cause-and-effect, practitioners seek to ultimately end the cycle of reincarnation and reach Nirvana. Buddhism is widespread in Vietnam, with estimates varying significantly due to cultural practices blending with formal affiliation, but generally, over half the population engages in Buddhist traditions, though formal registration is lower. Mahayana Buddhism dominates, mixed with ancestor worship, and is the country's second largest religion after folk beliefs.

C

C-130 Hercules: A four-engine turboprop military transport aircraft, built by Lockheed (now Lockheed Martin) in the U.S.A. Known for its versatility, ruggedness, and ability to operate from short, unprepared runways, it serves crucial roles in troop/cargo airlift, medevac, firefighting, aerial refueling, and special missions. Its high-wing design and rear loading ramp allow for easy transport of vehicles and supplies, making it a vital tactical aircraft for the past 70 years. Modern upgrades like the C-130J Super Hercules continue its legacy.

Cherry: A new soldier in Vietnam fresh from the United States. Also called a "boot," "newbie," or "FNG."

Chinook CH-47 Helicopter: A large, tandem-rotor, heavy-lift military transport helicopter made by Boeing in the U.S.A. It is renowned for its twin-rotor design, powerful engines, and versatility in moving troops, artillery, supplies, and equipment, as well as performing critical roles in medevac, disaster relief, and search and rescue. Its configuration eliminates the need for a tail rotor, allowing all power to focus on lift while providing excellent stability and a rear loading ramp.

Citadel in Huế: A massive, 19th-century fortified, walled city located on the northern bank of the Perfume River. Constructed between 1805 and 1832 during the Nguyễn Dynasty, it served as the political, administrative, and military center of Vietnam's last ruling monarchy.

Claymore Mine: A directional anti-personnel weapon, officially the M18A1, used for perimeter defense, ambushes, and against enemy infiltration. It fires hundreds of steel balls in a 60-degree forward arc, controlled remotely or via tripwire, featuring the iconic "FRONT TOWARD ENEMY" marking. It allowed U.S. and allied soldiers to protect bases and set traps from a safe distance.

Coconut Boat: A small, round, traditional bamboo and coconut leaf basket boat (thúng chai) used for fishing and tourist rides, especially in Hội An.

Compartmentalization: A psychological defense mechanism used to separate intense emotions, trauma, or personal life from operational duties, allowing soldiers to maintain focus in high-stress, life-threatening, or chaotic situations. Fear, pain, or conflicting moral dilemmas are "locked away" in order to prioritize a mission's success.

Concertina Wire: A spiraled, razor-sharp, steel-coiled fence-like obstacle that expands like an accordion to entangle enemy personnel and vehicles. It is primarily used to fortify perimeters, channel enemies into kill zones, and in multiple layers to surround and protect bases.

Confucianism: An ethical and philosophical system founded in China by Confucius (c. 551–479 BCE) that emphasizes moral uprightness, social harmony, respect for elders, and proper conduct through virtues like benevolence, righteousness, and propriety. It focuses on creating a stable society through ethical leadership and strong family bonds, and has influenced East Asian governance and social norms for millennia. The "golden rule" (also called the "silver rule") derives from Confucius' principle of restraint, empathy and reciprocity: Do not impose on others what you do not wish for yourself.

D

Dioxins: Persistent, toxic pollutants formed as byproducts of industrial processes (like waste incineration and paper bleaching) and some natural events (like wildfires and volcanoes), accumulating in the fatty tissues of animals and humans, primarily causing cancer, reproductive/developmental issues, immune damage, and hormone interference through contaminated food. The highly toxic dioxin compound TCDD was a dangerous contaminant in Agent Orange, an herbicide used during the War.

DMZ: An acronym for **Demilitarized Zone**. The geographical area separating North and South Vietnam.

Dug In (or Dig in): Having established a defensive position.

Dustoff or Dusty: Huey helicopters that provided transport to the closest in-theater hospital. Named for the dust it kicks up when taking off or landing, and part of the call sign for medevac missions. Crews typically consisted of two pilots, a medic, and a crew chief. Not to be confused with the M42 "Duster" anti-aircraft gun (so named because it turned enemies to dust).

E

Enlisted Personnel: In the Vietnam War, enlisted personnel formed the vast majority of the force, conducting combat, maintenance, and logistical tasks, while junior officers (lieutenants/captains) led them in the field. Due to high-risk roles like platoon leaders and pilots, junior officers faced disproportionately high casualty rates. While average soldiers were younger, the officer-enlisted structure created both reliance and, at times, strained command relationships.

F

Firebases: Fire Support Bases (FSBs or FBs) were temporary, fortified positions providing 360-degree artillery support for infantry operations. These highly defended posts, which included artillery, bunkers, and landing zones, served as essential hubs for controlling surrounding territory.

Flak Jacket: A form of body armor designed to provide protection from case fragments from explosive weaponry, anti-aircraft artillery, grenades, and lower-level projectiles. These vests contained ballistic nylon, and were not designed to stop bullets.

FNG: An acronym for **Fucking New Guy**. The newcomer to a unit, aircraft, or ship. Nearly always the target of relentless teasing and ridicule. Also called a "boot," "newbie," or "cherry."

FOB: An acronym for **Forward Operating Base**. A smaller base forward from the main base, usually with fewer amenities and only basic provisions, used to support tactical operations.

Foo Dog or Fu Dog: A Chinese-style guardian lion statue placed at the entrance of temples, palaces, and other important buildings. Typically placed in pairs to represent the yin and yang, with the male on the right and the female on the left, and believed to ward off evil spirits and attract good fortune and prosperity.

Free-Fire Zone: A designated area where any person or structure was considered hostile and subject to artillery and airstrike attacks without authorization. While the intent of the policy was for civilians to be evacuated, that often did not happen efficiently, either because they were not notified, refused to leave their ancestral lands, or were trapped, leading to high civilian casualties. Often used as a synonym for "Kill Zone," although the terms technically differ.

Freedom Bird: The aircraft that brought a service member home at the end of their tour of duty.

G

Gautama, Siddhartha: The founder of Buddhism, who renounced his life as a prince to become the Buddha, or "Enlightened One" through meditation. He discovered the path to end the cycle of human suffering and desires, teaching the Four Noble Truths (foundational teachings of Buddhism) to others.

GI: An acronym now generally referring to **Government Issue** or **General Issue**, although the term originates from **Galvanized Iron**. It refers to equipment, supplies, or belonging to the U.S. military, and also refers to a member of the U.S. Armed Forces.

GI Bill: A comprehensive package of education, housing, and training benefits provided by the VA to service members, veterans, and their dependents.

Gooks: A derogatory term and racial slur often used by U.S. troops for the Việt Cộng; sometimes used for any Vietnamese person.

Grunt: A slang term, often used as a badge of honor, for a combat infantry troop. The term gained widespread usage during the Vietnam War to describe those performing physically demanding ground operations.

Guerrilla Warfare: Unofficial military forces which incorporate surprise attacks, ambushes, and hit-and-run tactics to harass, delay, and disrupt a larger, conventional enemy. Guerillas will incorporate asymmetric tactics against superior forces, blend with the local population, and achieve objectives by inflicting casualties or disrupting supply lines rather than seizing and holding territory. During the Vietnam War, the Việt Cộng used guerrilla warfare.

H

Hamburger Hill: Referring to both the place and 10-day battle that occurred from May 10-20, 1969 between the U.S. Army and ARVN forces against the NVA. The hill's official name is Đồi A Bia and it is located in central Vietnam near its western border with Laos. Although the hill had little strategic value, U.S. command ordered its capture by a frontal assault, only to abandon it soon after and have it recaptured by the NVA. Approximately 70-72 U.S. soldiers died, with 372 to over 400 wounded. The battle caused a controversy among the U.S. armed services, politicians, and the American public. The name Hamburger Hill is derived from the bloody wounds and casualties that occurred during the battle.

Hanoi Hilton: A nickname for **Hỏa Lò Prison**, the most notorious North Vietnamese prison for U.S. prisoners of war.

Hercules or Herc: A colloquial nickname for the Lockheed C-130 transport plane.

Hồ Chí Minh: A Vietnamese Marxist-Leninist revolutionary and statesman who led the independence movement against French colonial rule and later became the first President of North Vietnam (Democratic Republic of Vietnam) from 1945 until his death. Although he passed away in 1969, the forces he helped establish ultimately unified the country under communist rule in 1975.

Hồ Chí Minh Trail: A crucial logistical network of paths and trails throughout the peninsula used by North Vietnamese forces to transport soldiers, weapons, and supplies from North Vietnam to the South, often to the Việt Cộng.

Huey: The Bell UH-1 Iroquois, or "Huey," was a multipurpose helicopter used by all service branches to transport troops, materials, and casualties, and sometimes provided reconnaissance, fire support, or was used to spray Agent Orange and other defoliants.

Hypervigilance: A trauma response causing a state of heightened alertness and constantly scanning for threats. Hypervigilance causes irritability, anxiety, overreacting to stimuli (like loud sounds), difficulty concentrating, and physical tension (like pounding heart, sweating). Stemming from experiences like combat or abuse, it can severely impact daily life, leading to social avoidance and relationship strain, but can often be managed with intense therapy.

I

In-country: A term for an American service member currently serving in Vietnam.

Indochina: The mainland region of Southeast Asia, encompassing present-day Vietnam, Cambodia, Laos, Thailand, Myanmar, and peninsular Malaysia, though often focusing on the former French Indochina (Vietnam, Cambodia, Laos). The term highlights the cultural blending of Indian and Chinese civilizations and also refers to the French colonial territory. Today, the broader area is usually called Mainland Southeast Asia, while "Indochina" often evokes its history, culture, and French colonial past.

J

Jarhead: A slang term for a Marine, often associated with their high and tight haircuts (resembling a jar lid). The term originated in World War II, referring to how a Marine's head looked sticking out of the high-collared blue dress uniform.

K

Kill Zone: A tactical, temporary area in an ambush where enemy forces are trapped. Often used as a synonym for "Free-Fire Zone," although the terms technically differ.

KP: An acronym for **Kitchen Patrol** or **Kitchen Police**. Unfavorable duty given to junior service members or assigned as a disciplinary measure for minor infractions. Also known as mess hall duty.

L

Liberty: A term used by U.S. troops for time off.

LRRP: Pronounced *lurp*, an acronym for **Long-Range Reconnaissance Patrol**. A small and specialized group that traveled deep into enemy territory to gather intelligence, rescue downed air crews, and engage the enemy as needed.

M

Mad Minute: A defensive tactic where all soldiers on a firebase or perimeter opened fire simultaneously for roughly one minute to test weapons and deter enemy attacks. It acted as a display of fire superiority, and often occurred at dusk or dawn.

Mamma San (or mamasan): A pidgin term used by American service personnel for older Vietnamese women who worked as housekeepers, laundresses, ("hooch maids"), or mess hall staff on the bases. Papa San or papasan was the male counterpart.

Medal of Honor: The highest U.S. military decoration for valor, awarded by the President for conspicuous gallantry and intrepidity "above and beyond the call of duty" in combat. As of early 2026, 3,547 individuals have received the decoration since its inception in 1861.

Mess/Mess Hall: Food hall or cafeteria. Also called chow hall.

Moral Injury: Deep psychological distress from violating, witnessing, or failing to prevent acts that oppose one's core moral beliefs, leading to intense guilt, shame, betrayal, and spiritual crisis. Moral injury stems from actions (or inactions) like causing harm, failing to protect, or being betrayed by leaders, and impacts self-worth, trust, and relationships. It is distinct from PTSD (which is fear-based), though they often co-occur.

MOS: (**Military Occupational Specialty**)**:** A primary assigned job in the U.S. Marine Corps and U.S. Army.

MP: An acronym for **Military Police**.

N

Napalm: A weaponized mixture of chemicals created by DOW Chemical, designed to create a highly flammable and gelatinous firebomb fuel-gel mixture. About 352,000 tons of U.S. napalm bombs were dropped in Vietnam between 1963 and 1973. The U.S. Air Force and Navy used napalm to firebomb enemy troops, tanks, buildings, jungles, and railroad tunnels. It was also used by U.S. troops to extend flamethrower range to 150 yards. As well as its tactical effects, napalm was used psychologically to break enemy morale by inflicting physical harm, destroying infrastructure, and spreading fear.

NLF: An acronym for **National Liberation Front**, a communist political movement formed in 1960 to overthrow the South Vietnamese government. The NLF is the political arm of the PLAF (People's Liberation Armed Forces), and their guerrilla fighters were usually referred to as the Việt Cộng.

NVA: An acronym for **North Vietnamese Army.** Also referred to as **PAVN**, acronym for **People's Army of Vietnam**. Both refer to the regular military of North Vietnam, established in 1950 and led by the Communist Party. Primarily composed of professional, committed soldiers, the NVA was a distinct, more conventional force than their NLF/Việt Cộng allies.

O

OTSD/CTSD: An acronym for **Ongoing/Continuous Traumatic Stress Disorder,** describing a chronic condition experienced by those living under ongoing, realistic, and often immediate threats to their safety—such as in war zones, chronic violence, or extreme poverty. The condition differs from PTSD, which is rooted in past trauma. While sufferers are in danger, this does not necessarily mean they are in constant danger, but rather that they live in conditions where danger is unpredictable and ever-present. Sufferers include caregivers and family members of those caring for or living with people who suffer from PTSD and other conditions.

P

Pagoda: A tiered tower with multiple eaves common in Buddhist traditions. Originating from the Indian stupa, pagodas typically serve as sacred, often multi-story shrines to house relics or scriptures, symbolizing the five elements: earth, water, fire, wind, and sky.

Paris Peace Accords: The 1973 agreement that effectively ended direct U.S. involvement in the Vietnam War.

Phở: Pronounced *fuh*, a fragrant noodle soup consisting of a slow-simmered broth, flat rice noodles (bánh phở), various cuts of meat, herbs and spices, and fresh vegetable garnishes. It is the national dish of Vietnam, and can be eaten any time of day, especially for breakfast.

Point Man, or Walking Point: The dangerous position at the front of a group of advancing troops. They were often the first to encounter the enemy, traps, and other hazards.

POW/MIA: Acronyms for Prisoner of War/Missing in Action. American or allied soldiers who were captured as prisoners were designated as Prisoners of War. After the War, many POWs who had gone missing would be classified as MIA.

PTSD: An **acronym for Post-Traumatic Stress Disorder**. As defined by the VA, it is a mental health condition derived from experiencing or witnessing severe trauma, such as combat or assault. Symptoms include flashbacks, nightmares, avoidance, irritability, hypervigilance, and detachment, which can disrupt daily life and emerge weeks, months, or years later.

Q

Quan Âm: The Vietnamese name for the bodhisattva of compassion and mercy, revered across East Asian Buddhism as a motherly figure who hears the cries of the suffering world, and often depicted holding an inverted vase (to signify the pouring of divine nectar to cleanse and purify the world) or with twelve arms (to signify her ability to help many people). Quan Âm represents unconditional love, and offers protection, spiritual guidance, and fertility. She is one of Vietnam's most beloved deities, with shrines found in homes, businesses, street corners, and temples throughout Vietnam.

R

R&R: An acronym for Rest and Recuperation, or a short leave.

REMF: An acronym for Rear Echelon Motherfucker. A derogatory term referring to someone who served in "rear" areas away from the fighting.

Reservist: A part-time service member in the U.S. Armed Forces who combines civilian life with military duty, training one weekend a month and two weeks a year, while remaining ready for deployment in national emergencies or wartime to supplement active-duty forces. Approximately 6,000 U.S. Army Reservists were mobilized for the Vietnam War, with about 3,500 deploying, mostly following the 1968 Tết Offensive. While President Johnson initially avoided a large-scale reserve call-up, reservists played crucial roles in transport, combat support, and engineering units rather than direct infantry combat.

Ruck/Rucksack: A lightweight backpack issued to infantry troops. Once filled with necessary resources such as water, food, clothes, weapons, ammo, and hand grenades, "rucks" could weigh up to 85 lbs.

S

Scrub: An often inexperienced, or low-ranking soldier or Marine.

Slopchute: Marine Corps slang for an often temporary, on-base enlisted club, or off-base shack bar near the base, both serving cheap beer.

Spider Hole: A foxhole just large enough for one troop to crouch into before covering the top of the hole with a camouflaged cover and staking out, waiting for movement, and observing enemy forces.

Spooky: The AC-47 gunship that proved fixed-wing planes (as opposed to rotary-wing like helicopters) had a place in providing close-air support in combat. The Spooky used side-firing guns to provide accurate, devastating fire while circling a target.

SVA: An acronym for **South Vietnamese Army,** commonly called **ARVN (Army of the Republic of [South] Vietnam).**

Swoop: Marine Corps slang for going on "liberty," typically leaving immediately after duties conclude on a Friday and returning Sunday night or early Monday.

T

TAD: An acronym for **Temporary Additional (or Active) Duty** away from one's permanent station, particularly for Navy and Marine Corps personnel. These assignments, lasting up to 189 days, are often for specialized roles, including combat support, intelligence, or technical training.

Taoism (or Daoism): An ancient philosophy and religion originating in China, whose core beliefs center on living in harmony with the Tao (the natural way of the Universe) through simplicity, authenticity, and spontaneity. Taoists emphasize balance (yin/yang), humility, compassion, and frugality, avoid harm, and aim for inner peace and alignment with nature, often through practices like meditation and Tai Chi.

Tết: (Tết Nguyên Đán): Vietnam's most important traditional holiday occurring in late January or early February, celebrating the Lunar New Year and the arrival of spring. Tết focuses on family reunions, honoring ancestors, and welcoming new beginnings with wishes of luck, health, and prosperity.

Tết Offensive: A major campaign of the War, marked by surprise attacks launched by the NVA and the Việt Cộng against the South Vietnamese Army and the United States Armed Forces and their allies. The attack occurred on military and civilian command and control centers throughout South Vietnam during the lunar new year (Tết) truce of January 30-31, 1968, when most ARVN personnel were on leave, and marked a major escalation of the War.

Tunnel Rats: American, Australian, and New Zealand combat engineers who explored, cleared, and destroyed the Việt Cộng's underground tunnel networks. Tunnel rats were generally men of smaller stature who were able to maneuver in the narrow tunnels. Considered among the most dangerous jobs in the War, they operated alone or in in small teams, facing traps, snakes, and armed enemy fighters in pitch-black, narrow spaces using only a flashlight, pistol, and knife (many later added a bayonet).

U

UNESCO World Heritage Site: Designated sites (spanning 1,248 locations across 170 countries as of July 2025) recognized for having "outstanding universal value" to humanity. These sites, classified as cultural, natural, or mixed, are protected under a 1972 international treaty for conservation and, in some cases, tourism. Vietnam boasts eight UNESCO sites, five of which our group visited: Hạ Long Bay, Tràng An Landscape Complex, Complex of Huế Monuments, Hội An Ancient Town, and the Imperial Citadel of Thăng Long in Hà Nội.

USO: An acronym for **United Service Organizations**, a private, non-profit charitable corporation which provided vital morale-boosting services in war zones for U.S. troops during the Vietnam War. Centers offered phone calls to family, helpful support staff, air-conditioned lounges, and famous celebrity entertainment "camp shows." These centers, operated and staffed by all-female volunteers, became essential safe havens, especially as non-combat areas became increasingly unsafe.

V

VA: An acronym for **U.S Department of Veterans Affairs**, a cabinet-level federal agency providing comprehensive, lifelong benefits, healthcare, and cemetery services to military veterans, their families, and survivors. It is the second-largest federal agency, and operates through three main administrations: the Veterans Health Administration (VHA), Veterans Benefits Administration (VBA), and National Cemetery Administration (NCA). The VA's mission is to fulfill President Lincoln's promise "to care for him who shall have borne the battle, and for his widow, and his orphan."

The VA is comprised of:

- Healthcare (VHA): Operates one of the nation's largest integrated healthcare networks, providing medical services, nursing homes, and clinics to over nine million veterans.
- Benefits (VBA): Manages disability compensation, education assistance (GI Bill), vocational rehabilitation, home loan guarantees, and life insurance.
- Burial and Memorial (NCA): Provides burial and memorial services at 135 national cemeteries.
- Structure: The VA employs over 350,000 staff, including specialized medical professionals.

VFW: An acronym for **Veterans of Foreign Wars of the United States,** a nonprofit, federally chartered organization founded in 1899 for honorably discharged veterans who served in combat or foreign conflicts. It acts as a major advocacy group, aiding veterans with benefits, supporting military families, and promoting community service. Its mission is to foster camaraderie among veterans of overseas conflicts; serve veterans, the military, and communities; and advocate on behalf of all veterans.

Việt Cộng (also **Việt Communist; VC, Cong, NLF): **The communist guerrilla forces in South Vietnam; a pejorative term given to the National Liberation Front's armed forces and coined by the ARVN. Sometimes referred to as "gooks," "bad guys," or "Victor Charlie" (or just "Charlie") by American and allied troops.

Việt Minh: The independence movement that fought against French rule before the division of Vietnam.

Vietnamization: Nixon's policy to withdraw U.S. troops and transfer combat responsibility to the ARVN.

W

Watch Your Six: A phrase used by troops meaning to watch your back or stay vigilant for threats from behind. The "six" refers to the six o'clock position on a clock, which is directly behind you.

Willie Peter: A nickname for white phosphorus employed by the U.S. Military. *Note: Ed says that Willie Peter was developed in Hell. If you got it on you it stayed afire, burning through flesh. It was feared by all. I asked why they used the name Willie Peter, other than it having the same initials as white phosphorus. He said in the military, commands are always as short as possible under stressful situations. Hence Willie Peter is understood quicker than white phosphorus. Even a syllable matters, he stressed.*

The World: Military slang for the United States or life back home.

Recommendations for Further Reading

Spanish writer, poet, and playwright Miguel de Cervantes is best known for his novel *Don Quixote*. Although the book is a satirical literary masterpiece, I believe Cervantes's most profound message stems from one particular phrase: "The pen is the tongue of the mind." (Variations of this were also expressed, albeit more obscurely, by the Roman poet Horace.) In any case, the sentiment is that the pen can access what is otherwise hidden. This coincides with one of my own personal mantras: the pen says what the mouth cannot.

This concept is what first led me to embrace writing. As an adolescent, journaling and composing poems of my innermost fears and anguish allowed me to exorcise those feelings in a cathartic and constructive manner. And of course, I am not alone. Writing, music, visual art, and other creative endeavors have given humans the opportunity to express our full range of emotions—be it overzealous joy or blazing torment—without the destructive outcomes of less benign outlets.

I hope that my endeavor of writing this book—particularly transcribing, paraphrasing, and chronicling the interviews and experiences of veterans—has enabled them to express thoughts they may not have been able to voice previously.

Readers also benefit from the free rein of the pen by "hearing" the words inside a mind whose tongue cannot speak them. I urge you to continue reading books relating to the Vietnam War—be they history, memoirs, or novels—so that pens continue to speak and perceptive minds continue to be heard. Most importantly, doing so will enrich your personal awareness and understanding of a time period so vital to the United States, Vietnam, and their citizens.

History Titles:

Fire in the Lake, by Frances FitzGerald
The Long Reckoning, by George Black
Scorched Earth, by Fred A. Wilcox
Until the Last Gun is Silent, by Matthew F. Delmont

The Vietnam War, by Geoffrey Ward and Kenneth Burns (companion to the television series)
The Vietnam War: A Graphic History, by Dwight Jon Zimmerman
Vietnam: A History, by Stanley Karnow
Vietnam: A New History, by Christopher Goscha
We Were Soldiers Once…and Young, by Lt. General Harold G. Moore and Joseph Galloway

Autobiographies, Biographies, and Memoirs:

A Bright Shining Lie, by Neil Sheehan
Dispatches, by Michael Herr
The Education of Corporal John Musgrave, by John Musgrave
The Girl in the Picture, by Denise Chong
I Came Home, But It Wasn't Me: The Memoirs of a Vietnam Combat Veteran as a Recon Scout "LRRP," by Bruce Taneski
Lone Survivor, by Marcus Luttrell
A Rumor of War, by Philip Caputo
Secrets: A Memoir of Vietnam and the Pentagon Papers, by Daniel Ellsberg
A Vietcong Memoir, by Truong Nhu Tang
The War Within a War: The Black Struggle in Vietnam and at Home, by Wil Haygood
When Heaven and Earth Changed Places, by Le Ly Hayslip and Jay Wurts

Historical/Political Novels:

Fields of Fire, by James Webb
Matterhorn: A Novel of the Vietnam War, by Karl Marlantes
The Mountains Sing, by Nguyen Phan Que Mai
The Quiet American, by Graham Greene
The Sorrow of War, by Bao Nin
The Sympathizer, by Viet Thanh Nguyen
The Things They Carried, by Tim O'Brien
The Women, by Kristin Hannah
Why Are We in Vietnam? by Norman Mailer (allegorical)

Anthologies:

Free Fire Zone: Short Stories by Vietnam Veterans, edited by Wayne T. Karline, Basil T. Paquet, and Larry Rottmann

The Vietnam Reader, edited by Stewart O'Nan

Winning Hearts and Minds: War Poems by Vietnam Veterans, edited by Larry Rottmann, Jan Barry, and Basil T. Paquet

Acknowledgements

I am grateful to Senator Tom Carper for providing the foreword for this book, and to his executive assistant, Jacqueline Cameron, who facilitated the process. Senator Carper, who retired at the end of 2024, was the final serving Vietnam veteran in the U.S. Senate, and a champion for veterans throughout his political career. It is an honor to have him acknowledge this book.

I'd like to formally recognize all the veterans who traveled with us and endured my litany of questions during our multiple interview sessions, phone calls, and emails, and to thank them for sharing their war stories and experiences: Lou Garrison, Raymond Kennedy, Kevin Laughlin, Charles Walter, Ed Woods, and Mary Zelanis-Laughlin.

I'd also like to thank Mike Rans and Rick Storino, two veterans who did not join our trip but whose experiences were included to enhance our narrative.

To the spouses who joined the veterans on our trip, your longtime compassion, care, and unwavering support have not gone unnoticed: Karen Garrison, Agnes Walter, Fran Woods, and Mary Zelanis-Laughlin.

I'd like to send heartfelt thanks to my friend and contributor, Patrick Sullivan, DO, for the information he provided about his medical experience with veterans, PTSD, and alternative treatments. His contribution to this book presents readers with a clearer understanding of the profound psychological challenges faced by war veterans.

Fred Gray was able to identify the various tanks and armored vehicles in photos my dad and I took in Vietnam, as well as equipment in Vietnam War-era photographs. Fred served as a tank driver, gunner, and track commander in the War, and we are grateful for his service and the information he shared with us.

Bruce Taneski is a prolific author of war-related novels and a memoir of his own experiences as a Vietnam War recon scout. He and stand-up comic and novelist Andrew Bayroff both offered advice on the benefits and mechanics of self-publishing, and I made use of their combined wisdom.

I'd like to acknowledge the Vietnamese planner and guides who helped make our trip an unequivocal success and who also contributed to this narrative: Xuân Vũ Thành, Thế Đăng Anh, Anh-Cơ Nguyễn, and Thành Phạm. Their collective warmth and expertise will always be remembered.

My long-time friend and editor extraordinaire, Karen Nolan Visconti, volunteered her copy-editing services and narrative feedback to this book and has my sincere gratitude for her skill, analysis, and enthusiastic encouragement.

Another long-time friend, Mike Ripca, has graciously provided his design and layout expertise to this book, and I am eternally thankful for his professional expertise, advice, and friendship.

To my dear friend Brady Buck, your creative input and inspiration will always be remembered.

To my brother, Edward Woods III, who accompanied our father on his first return visit, thank you for your thoughtful feedback of that journey and overall support of this project.

I am grateful to my husband Ed and daughter Tara for putting up with the repeated delays of this book and my myriad of excuses. Thank you also, dear family, for enduring my sadness due to overwhelming war statistics and personal accounts, interspersed with random enthusiasm over things like tanks and helicopters.

To my mother, Fran Woods, whose enduring support and matriarchal grace and compassion are the cornerstone of our extended family.

Most of all, I'd like to thank my father, Ed Woods, for his contributions to this book, for allowing me to accompany him and his fellow veterans on the trip, and for trusting me with his War experiences and their subsequent life-long obstacles.

And to veterans of all wars, residing in all countries, may your sacrifices always be remembered and one day contribute to a more peaceful future where the young do not fight the battles of the old, and children always see the whole of their parents.

About the Authors and Contributor

Colleen Woods-Esposito

Colleen's career has spanned a multitude of ventures from graphic design and marketing to photography, journalism, and education. She now spends her time creating abstract drawings and paintings, reading dystopian novels and history, traveling near and far, honoring nature and the seasons, cooking for friends and family, walking through the woods with a camera, bingeing British mysteries, planting and growing, writing poetry and essays, and playing music at distasteful volumes. In essence, she's never bored.

Colleen holds a B.A. from Rowan University and an M.S. from Drexel University. She lives in rural South Jersey with her beloved husband Ed, daughter Tara, and very tolerant feline. This is her first book.

Ed Woods, Jr., USMC

After his separation from the Marine Corps in late 1967, Ed worked in a Glassboro, New Jersey factory as a machine operator and shift foreman. During the seventies and eighties, he supplemented his income by purchasing and managing properties and working part-time as a sports team and wedding photographer.

When the factory closed in the early nineties, Ed became a full-time professional photographer and also began writing for food magazines. Occasionally, he led photo tours to Europe, where he taught amateurs his love of travel photography. Ed still writes quarterly articles for a Schenectady, New York lifestyle magazine.

While photographing and interviewing luminaries such as Emeril Lagasse, Guy Fieri, and Mario Batali, Ed developed a fervent interest in creative cuisine, and still enjoys cooking on a daily basis.

As well as his own gastronomic creations, Ed and his wife Fran love traveling the world and savoring the cuisines of each destination. In addition to travel and food, Ed enjoys keeping fit and lounging by the poolside in his beautifully landscaped yard in Sewell, New Jersey.

Patrick Sullivan, DO

Dr. Patrick Sullivan is a board-certified emergency physician with over 20 years of clinical experience, including extensive work in both psychiatric and neurologic emergency departments. His background uniquely positions him to diagnose and treat a wide range of complex conditions, from mood and substance use disorders, to pain and neurologic emergencies such as stroke and intractable headaches.

In 2016, Dr. Sullivan founded *Initia Nova* (Latin for "new beginning"), one of the first medical practices on the East Coast to offer ketamine infusion therapy (KIT) for treatment-resistant depression. In 2017, he developed the ketamine-assisted psychotherapy program (KAP) for PTSD and other complex conditions. By 2018, *Initia Nova* began offering transcranial magnetic stimulation (TMS), and was among the first to implement accelerated theta burst protocols. Dr. Sullivan is one of a small number of physicians worldwide to combine ketamine with TMS for patients who have not responded to either treatment alone or even to electroconvulsive therapy (ECT).

Known for his innovative and holistic approach, Dr. Sullivan integrates metabolic health into personalized treatment protocols that support neuroplasticity, reduce inflammation, and promote long-term wellness. His programs for addiction, chronic pain, and treatment-resistant headaches combine ketamine, NAD+ infusions, TMS, nerve blocks, psychotherapy, lifestyle interventions, and targeted medications—offering new hope to those who have failed conventional therapies.

Dr. Sullivan and his team specialize in helping patients navigate some of the most difficult challenges, including depression, PTSD, OCD, addiction, and chronic pain, with compassion, expertise, and a commitment to whole-person healing.

www.ingramcontent.com/pod-product-compliance
Lightning Source LLC
LaVergne TN
LVHW010645110826
845149LV00014B/2955